GUARDIANS OF *the* REPUBLIC

REFLECTIONS ON THE BOOK

"Human dignity is the prerequisite of not only human rights but human existence itself. It needs to be protected, cherished and blossomed in every respect, in every form of governance. The onus becomes heavy on nations like India, which boast of liberal democracy and dynamic constitutionalism casting responsibility on all the pillars of the state. This is the profound and pervasive message, delivered very effectively, in this book authored by Dr Ashwani Kumar.

"In a powerful and thought-provoking exploration, the author delves into the complexities of human dignity, revealing its significance in shaping our lives, relationships, and societies. Dr Ashwani Kumar, a lawyer by profession who joined politics by choice, has rich experience in public life. He's the amalgam of a great jurist and exceptional politician who has excelled in both the fields, and that can be discerned from the variety of essays.

"With profound insights and compelling narratives, this book challenges us to re-examine our values and assumptions, and to recognize the inherent worth and dignity of every human being. It depicts the author's maturity and commitment to the cause and points out the significance of dignity in varied facets of life. An essential read for every right-minded citizen concerned with justice, equality, and human flourishing." – **Justice A.K. Sikri, Former Judge, Supreme Court of India, International Judge, Singapore International Commercial Court**

"In today's highly politicised world it has never been more important to understand the proper limits of the interaction between democratic pressure and judicial restraint on populism. This book provides a thoughtful and well-evidenced insight to these topics from a highly experienced senior lawyer and politician with first-hand experience of these issues. Though focused on India it carries important insights for other countries round the world." – **Lord Peter Goldsmith KC, Former Attorney General for England and Wales, Chair of European and Asian Litigation, Debevoise & Plimpton LLP**

"Hope is a precious commodity in these times of '*fracture and fear*'. This volume of essays upholds the Nehruvian vision of a liberal democratic republic in the face of the dismantling and capitulation of the institutional edifice of India's 'flailing' democracy. Eschewing political polemics, the writer-cum-poet-cum-jurist gently chides us for our 'collective and institutional failures to vindicate the vision of our founders'. Noting the global dimension of this challenge, he invites us, especially the political leaders, to rekindle a moral vision and act upon it, so as to affirm Sahir Ludhianvi's hope: '*woh subah kabhi to aayegi*'" – **Yogendra Yadav, Political activist and National Convenor, Bharat Jodo Abhiyaan**

"This is a must-read for anyone interested in the critical, continuing debate in India about the proper role of judges in India's constitutional democracy. Ashwani Kumar's anthology of essays is a learned, inspired, eloquent and, at times, poetic, vindication of the humanitarian role of the judicial arm of the state in defending fundamental human rights. His book critically examines important themes such as the Indian Supreme Court's invocation of the basic structure doctrine, the current threats to the presumption of innocence in an age of media prejudgment, and the prevalence of custodial torture by the police and other investigating agencies that was exposed by the recent judgment of the English High Court in the case of Bhandari." – **Edward Fitzgerald KC, Barrister, Founding Head of Doughty Street Chambers, London**

GUARDIANS OF *the* REPUBLIC

Essays on the Constitution, Justice, and the Future of Indian Democracy

ASHWANI KUMAR

Om Books International

First published in 2025 by

Om Books International

Corporate & Editorial Office
A-12, Sector 64, Noida 201 301
Uttar Pradesh, India
Phone: +91 120 477 4100
Email: editorial@ombooks.com
Website: www.ombooksinternational.com

Sales Office
107, Ansari Road, Darya Ganj,
New Delhi 110 002, India
Phone: +91 11 4000 9000
Fax: +91 11 2327 8091
Email: sales@ombooks.com
Website: www.ombooks.com

ISBN: 978-93-6395-397-0

Printed in India

Dedicated to the memory of Dr Manmohan Singh,
whose quiet dignity and nobility of purpose
elevated him above his exalted office

Contents

"A time for us someday there'll be
A new world, a world of shining hope for you and me"
—Eddie Snyder and Larry Ku

FOREWORD

Democracy is on trial, and it's for sensitive minds living in a system that continues to be rated as the best choice for governance to ask why. Is it that the elected in a democracy are being increasingly swayed by the temptations of concentrated power? Is it that the institutions of a civil society are seen as a hindrance to absolute power in the free world? When I reflect at the arc of ideas and arguments in Ashwani Kumar's new book, I feel that there is still hope because of writers who dare to question the transgressions of power. Scholar, eminent lawyer, jurist, parliamentarian and a former Union Minister, Kumar is one such writer.

What sets this collection of essays apart is their intellectual eclecticism. Kumar's insight into the interface between judiciary and political power is a reminder that an antagonistic relationship between the law and the legislature diminishes popular faith in the idea of democracy itself. The author's credentials as an uncompromising apostle of the rule of law shine through the narrative. If the crippling of institutions is one of the most shared profanities in polities where leaders maximise their power at the cost of civil liberties, Kumar provides the strongest advocacy for the restoration of institutional sanctity.

Kumar broadens his gaze, stretching from the devastation and dispossession of Gaza to the battlefields of Ukraine, to underline the failure of Western leadership in preserving the ideals of democracy. It is as if the whirl of history is so ferocious that the rulers of the world are still struggling to make sense of it—let alone manage it. An internationalist driven by national interest, Kumar refuses to let pessimism cloud his judgement. He offers a poetic remedy to the waywardness of the current global leadership: listen to "the hidden silences". There is no other way to unlock the conscience, he tells us.

Even as he elucidates on governance with a moral content, Kumar won't spare the contentious motifs of the zeitgeist. From the ethical challenges of AI to the dystopian promises of Big Tech, the thematic range of this book brings out Kumar's relentless engagement with a future that balances anxiety with hope, all the while maintaining his narrative elegance. His call for renewal is tempered with caution. In a world where the path to progress runs parallel to ideological extremism, Kumar, the good lawyer that he is, argues for the humanisation of development—and vice versa.

This is the work of a humanist steeped in the poetics of his cultural inheritance. Here is a writer who can quote Terry Eagleton and Allama Iqbal with the same sense of familiarity. He writes on politics with a literary flair; his scholarship exudes multiple cultural strains. This is a book written by someone who deeply cares for his country, and who values refined discourse as much as he appreciates the rewards of decency in politics. It brings back the lost decencies and dignities of public life. A former cabinet minister who is today unrestrained by the exigencies of realpolitik, Kumar declares his allegiance to the ideas of freedom. The well-chiselled words in this book are a validation: dissent alone redeems democracy.

M. Hamid Ansari,

Vice President of India, 2007–17

INTRODUCTION

This book presents a perspective on the failings and possibilities of Indian democracy. It carries forward the argument advanced in my two earlier publications: that democracy, dignity and freedom are secured when asserted by the people and that "every state lives upon the character of its citizens". A corollary of this view is that those who manage the institutions of democracy, including the judges, are not unaffected by the dominant tides and currents of the day. Therefore, their role in the deepening of democracies is limited and mixed. The evolution of India's constitutional jurisprudence and the inter-institutional contestation confirm this proposition.

The institutions which undergird India's democracy face the enormous challenge of responding to popular aspirations of a rising nation, shackled with the baggage of historical inequities. Since the constitutional power structures and the exercise of institutional power impact the course of our future, the inter-institutional tension for recognition and relevance demands sagacious management. It is argued that a harmonious exercise of dispersed sovereign power will best advance the goals of India's dignitarian democracy.

The echo of the 2014 transformative moment has since been heard loud and clear in the workings of our constitutional institutions. The burden of these reflections is to draw attention to challenges that confront India's liberal democracy in a fundamentally altered political landscape and to some of the worrisome aberrations of our democratic compact. The essays focus on the role of the judicial branch in its interface with executive power, in the framework of a stressed democracy. In my book, *Hope in a Challenged Democracy*, published in 2016, I argued that Indian democracy stands denuded of its moral appeal, and democratic institutions stand eroded from within. I repeat what I had stated then, that "we owe it to future generations to ensure that our parliamentary democracy is not held hostage to perennial conflict and a debilitating competition for power without high purpose".

Instances of capitulation of democratic institutions in times of test have deepened the fault lines of India's flailing democracy. The Opposition, claiming that its voice is not heard in the corridors of power, has repeatedly resorted to judicial remedies, leading to an ongoing debate about the boundaries of judicial review in a parliamentary democracy. The ruling party parliamentarians have, in recent days, questioned the Supreme Court's decision regarding the exercise of sovereign power by the governors and the President, as stretching the limits of judicial review beyond the constitutional mandate. Although the rationale of the Court's judicial review jurisdiction for "enforcing the restraints of the Constitution" is generally conceded as an "auxiliary precaution" against majoritarian impulses, fixing its limits in a parliamentary democracy has been a subject of an unending debate. Laments about the "juridification of politics" and "politicisation of the judiciary" have kept the issue alive. This has been discussed in an updated essay, considering the importance of the subject in relation to structures and processes of democratic governance.

The book reiterates the imperative of remaining true to democratic values anchored in the rule of law and deference to the moral sensitivities of the people. These cannot be compromised at the altar of political exigencies or suborned to the passions of the mob. Thus, the presumption of innocence in criminal investigations, a recognised human right, cannot be compromised to satisfy the cacophony of the crowds nor made hostage to media trials interdicted by the Constitution. Neither can we forget that law enforcers cannot become agents of injustice, as demonstrated in recurring instances of abuse of power. Concerns have also been expressed about the Supreme Court's failure to enforce several of its edicts and some of the core constitutional values. These include the Court's failure to facilitate a comprehensive law against custodial torture. As the highest constitutional court, the apex court is more than a propounder of the Constitution or narrator of constitutional principles. Its mandate is to vindicate constitutional rights in practice, deriving strength from the popular trust in its moral and intellectual integrity to enlist the community's willing allegiance. Indeed, the Court's pre-eminent role in the life of the nation depends not on what it says but does with what it says[1].

However, these concerns do not discount the Court's progressive record in the evolution of the jurisprudence of rights "rights that elevate the law"- and the principle of accountability in the exercise of constitutional power. Its orders proscribing "Bulldozer Justice", the exoneration of Professor Saibaba and granting bail to several accused on account of an unconscionably long incarceration, earlier missteps notwithstanding, are a robust affirmation of the Constitution's libertarian

1. Professor Karl Llewellyn, *The Bramble Bush: On our Law and its Study*, Louisiana, New Orleans, Quid Pro Books, 2012, cited in Professor Upendra Baxi, 'Basic Structure: A Solid Foundation or Fragile Bastion' in 'Doctrine of Basic Structure: Revisiting Kesavananda Bharati Verdict' on its 50th Anniversary, National Law University and Judicial Academy, Assam, 2024.

philosophy. The judgment of the apex court regarding the constitutional role of governors in a federal and representative democracy in the context of inordinate delay in granting assent to bills passed by the Tamil Nadu Legislative Assembly, subserves the principle of cooperative federalism and representative democracy, even though it can be critiqued as an exercise in stretched constitutionalism, as far as its ruling in relation to the exercise of presidential prerogative is concerned. The decision of the Bombay High Court on the freedom of speech in Kunal Kamra's case, an essay in judicial statesmanship, is defined by reasoned justice and fairness. Recent decisions of the Court in Pratapgarhi[2] and the Thug Life case[3] decisively affirm the constitutional right to free speech.

Yet, while the nation prizes the freedom of the press as an assurance against oppression and injustice, the manifest capitulation of the fourth estate to government diktats, exceptions apart, is a discomforting truth. Television news, mostly "dumbed down and tarted up", can hardly claim to mirror the nation's conscience. Pervasive media trials impinging on the first principles of justice, invariably compromise the cherished constitutional right to privacy and dignity. We know that the right of expression has meaning only if it enables

2. Imran Pratapgarhi v. State of Gujarat 2025 INSC 410

3. Sri M. Mahesh Reddy v. State of Karnataka & Ors. (W.P.(C) No. 575/2025)

the discovery of truth through the "fullest and freest comparison of opposite opinions", in the "marketplace of ideas". And, democracy can survive only as long as conscientious dissenters can have their voice heard without fear of reprisals. In a situation where both privately owned and government-controlled media are amenable to influence, public opinion is susceptible to manipulation by those in authority through journalists and television anchors, who now combine the roles of the presenter, prosecutor and the judge.

A chapter on the failure of leadership of the Western democracies to stand up for principles and prevent hostilities between Israel and Iran, in Gaza and Ukraine, focuses on the need for transformative leadership in the current global context. The eulogies in the book salute virtuous leadership and affirm the oft-cited eloquence of Justice Joseph Story, a distinguished American judge, that "republics are created by the virtue, public spirit, and intelligence of the citizens. They fall when the wise are banished from public councils." Indeed, the exertions of the tallest amongst us have shown that the ideal of establishing a truly empowering democracy in which "justice is the first virtue of social institutions" is not beyond us. This can be ensured by magnanimous leadership and an unswerving commitment to the high principles that define the republic. Democratic leadership is about the pursuit of human dignity and an unfailing commitment to helm politics inspired by high purpose. It is about shunning the extremes and a just exercise of power to stabilise a society under stress. The tribute to some of the towering leaders of our times included in the book is a reiteration of my belief that democracy and its ideals, anywhere in the world, can be powered only by men and women who can rise above themselves to "listen creatively to the hidden silences..."

The acclaimed poet Allama Iqbal's eloquent verse defines the qualities of leadership in all ages thus:

nigah buland sukhan dil-navāz jaañ pur-soz
yahī hai rakht-e-safar mīr-e-kārvāñ ke liye

(soaring vision, dulcet speech, a feeling heart,
that is all. the baggage of the caravan's chief/leader)

Clearly, in times of "fracture and fear", the question of leadership assumes a special significance. Democracies demand leadership that can rise above "the compromise and littleness of most lives", invest politics with the loftiness of purpose. A case for accountability of power and its benign exercise demands leadership that can energise the processes of democracy. With the recurring abuse of power by persons unwilling to tame their ambitions to the higher purpose of their calling, and expediency repeatedly prevailing over principle in the corridors of power, the legitimacy of democratic processes is suspect. The apparent dichotomy between practice and precept by those asserting their claim to leadership of the nation is a continuing indictment of our politics. The urgency to recompose politics and right our priorities is a challenge for those who aspire to lead the nation. Will reason redeem politics and produce leadership that can unite political ambition with passion for justice? It is the penultimate question that lingers in the interstices of the book.

A piece on the ethical boundaries of Artificial Intelligence is included as a critical subject impacting the evolution of democracy and is an iteration of the imperative of preserving the core democratic values of privacy, dignity and freedom in the digital age. Driven by the inevitability of AI's pervasive entry into our lives, the need for a deeper reflection of its impact on humanity is self-evident. The fact that passionate propounders of AI such as Elon Musk have cautioned against "summoning the devil without a kill switch", a concern shared by Mark Zuckerberg and Steve Wozniak amongst others, must awaken us to the urgency of serious reflection on how to preserve "the hidden realm of the mind from which emotions emerge, from which inspiration flows, from which our desires pulse—the subjective part of the human spirit that makes each of us ineluctably who we are".

While continuing the pursuit of scientific advancement, we must pause to ponder ways in which the technical revolutionary stride can undermine democracy and its ethical underpinnings. Sarah Wynn-Williams' book, *Careless People*, is an exposé of Facebook's ethical flexibility and complicity in furthering the surveillance and censorship agenda of the Chinese communist party, its indifference to the genocide of the Rohingya in Myanmar and its role in the US presidential election of 2016. The book is a renewed wake-up call against the unfettered power of mega technology companies to undermine human rights and derail the course of democracy across the world. Laila Lalami's *The Dream Hotel* (Pantheon, 2025) is a chilling depiction of a possible dystopian future of the marginalised in the world driven by AI. Such thoughtful insights on the impact of AI in reflecting and shaping the quotidian reality compel us to ask whether man's creation can be allowed to challenge the supremacy of the creator, in which he will cease to be the "measure of all things".

The assertion of a moral vision to regulate the use of technology, such as would advance the cause of a virtuous and happy society, is an urgent imperative. The English literary theorist and public intellectual, Terry Eagleton's words of caution in relation to a sense of seductive self-assurance are compelling, and I quote: "An inflated self-belief can earn its calamitous comeuppance, which caused the ancient Greeks to shudder and look fearfully to the skies". Sigmund Freud's worrisome caution is apt. The philosopher had warned: "Human beings have made such strides in controlling the forces of nature that with the help of these forces, they will have no difficulty in exterminating one another, down to the last man. They know this, and it is this knowledge that accounts for much of their present disquiet, unhappiness and anxiety…"[4] German physicist Georg Christoph Lichtenberg's prophecy, "who knows in centuries to come there will not be universities for reestablishing our former ignorance", has deep resonance today amongst thinkers grasping with the adverse humanitarian consequences of a vastly disruptive technological revolution. The Spanish philosopher Ortegay Gasset's profound articulation of the dilemma of man in confrontation with his reality is even more valid today than when it first captured the popular imagination. "We live at a time," he wrote, "when man believes himself fabulously capable of creation, but he does not know what to create. Lord of all things, he is not Lord of himself. He feels lost amid his own abundance. With more means at its disposal, more knowledge, more technique than ever, it turns out

4. Sigmund Freud, *Civilization and Its Discontents*, 1930

that the world today goes the same way as the worst of worlds that have been; it simply drifts."[5]

A nation ranked amongst the lowest in the Global Development Index, Global Happiness Index, Global Hunger Index, Gender Inequality Index, Global Multidimensional Power Index, at 151 out of 180 countries in the World Press Freedom Index and described as a "flawed" or "hybrid" democracy in the recent Global Democracy Index of The *Economist*, can hardly claim to be a role model for democracies across the world. Electoral exercises have little value without governance and policies yielding justice and dignity for all.

In its entirety, the book underscores the need for a politics of national renewal, premised on the return to reason and civility in the conduct of politics that espouses human dignity as the preeminent constitutional value. This would require a disciplined political discourse focused on the ills that plague Indian democracy, not on venting personal animosities. The concerns expressed are a reminder of the infirmities of our challenged democracy that need to be addressed to realise the nation's grand ambition and are inspired by actual happenings, lending them their immediate significance. Indeed, events "shape the land and the

5. José Ortega y Gasset, *The Revolt of the Masses*, London, 1951

people who live in it". The readings in the book ought to be tested on the touchstone of the tone and temper of our times, defined by the "decline of tolerance and the rise of moral absolutism". The critique of our collective and institutional failures to vindicate the vision of our founders is an exercise in self-censure, driven by a duty to contribute to a rational comprehension of the unpalatable truths of the republic. The stated and implicit assumption of these writings is that a conscientious adherence to principle and willingness to speak truth to power can alone enlighten the democratic path to a better world.

Our politics cannot be morally neutral, nor can the conscience of the nation be silenced. Readings and reflection that have inspired these writings have convinced me further that the "moral history of humanity" will examine the role of thinkers in shaping the world, not by their neutrality in discussing "the transvaluation of values" but by their political activism in translating their recipes for a world in which the universal ideal of the good and a sense of "belonging to all humanity" will prevail over narrower identities and the various "particularisms". The intellectual cannot set himself apart from the activists inspired by him. Viewed thus, politics as the highest form of public service must inspire the active participation of intellectuals. And leaders pursuing a moral cause, rising above the self and pettiness anchored in vicious animosities, are entitled to respect regardless of their political leanings. Reasons for the impoverishment of politics need to be fearlessly articulated and addressed through demonstrable corrective action by political parties leading the charge. Democratic politics is not about pontification. It is about a superior and a visibly inspiring political morality in action. These meditations have reinforced my belief that there is no freedom when basic human rights are at the sufferance of those in authority and the processes of governance are hostage to the whims of the powerful.

Realisation of the ideal of a truly liberal democracy being a work in progress, the process of questioning and correcting its aberrations must remain an unrelenting endeavour. Prime Minister Atal Bihari Vajpayee's evocative verse about scripting his destiny through a sustained resolve mirrors the nation's collective aspiration.

hār nahin mānūn gā, rār nahin thānūn gā
kāl ke kapāl par likhta mitātā hūn
gītnayā gātā hūn

(I will not give up, nor will I accept defeat,
On the forehead of time, I write and erase,
I sing a new song.)

The nation must indeed find its song of resurgence. It is incumbent upon us, therefore, to proclaim aloud that a manufactured imagination, indifferent to the "sleep of reason", mounted on visceral hostilities, promoting discord over dialogue and indifferent to the heightened social and economic inequities, does not accord with the promise of a representative democracy founded on empathy and fraternity. The "pauperisation of the weak in the interests of the powerful…", the deepening of social and communal divides and the coercive propensities of the state represent a damning denouement of our democratic pretensions.

The lives of the multitude tormented by heart-rending penury and hopelessness mock Tocqueville's idea of democracy in which "…the people hover above the entire life of the state … as the cause and end of all things…" Yet, this ennobling idea must remain our perennial inspiration for establishing a just democratic order in which liberty, equality and fraternity as conjoint and sacrosanct values command our unconditional fealty. To the practicalists, one may say that a cynical indifference to humanitarianism as a guiding philosophy of democracy is tantamount to a retreat from an inquiry into the foundational premises of the Indian state. This would obscure our understanding of the present and possibilities for the future.

This book is about hope for a just social and political order captured in Sahir Ludhianvi's immortal verse:

Bīteñge kabhī to din ākhir ye bhuukh ke aur bekārī ke
Tūteñge kabhī to būt ākhir daulat kī ijāra-dārī ke
Haq māñgne vāloñ ko jis din suulī na dikhāī jāegī
Jab paap gharauñde phūteñge jab zulm ke bandhan tūteñge

Jab ek anokhī duniyā kī buniyād uthāī jāegī
Jab dhartī karvat badlegī, jab qaid se
Qaidī chhūteñge, woh subah kabhi to ayegi
Us subah ko ham hī lāeñge vo subah hamīñ se aaegī

(The days of hunger and joblessness will be over one day.
The monopoly of wealth will be shattered someday,
And the day will come when those who demand their rights,
Will not be condemned to the gallows,
When the houses of sin will crumble,
When the chains of oppression will be broken,
When the foundation of a new order will be laid,
When the world will take a new turn,
and the imprisoned will walk free,
that dawn heralding a new beginning will at last

come and,
We will be the ones to bring that dawn.)

The universal resonance of this powerful imagery of an unjust society validates the thought that it is "…the adventure of poetry, not the closure of philosophy, that most truly reflects the human condition".

Wisened by history and empowered by reason, it is for us, as inheritors of a free nation, to ensure that a democracy envisioned to enrich lives does not waste itself through unconscionable acquiescence in injustice, which impairs self-esteem and human dignity irremediably. There is no reason for hopelessness because history is about hope and its lights and not only about its "long shadows".

People decide the truth of their lived reality in the image of their experiences, and as Frantz Fanon, reminding us of the logic of the unending struggle for inter-generational equities, proclaimed, "each generation must discover its mission, fulfil it or betray it".[6] While succeeding generations will navigate their own reality, the essence of a liberal constitutional democracy, viz, the accountability of power to the prescribed means and the ends of its exercise, must remain inviolate. We can

6. Frantz Fanon, *The Wretched of the Earth*, 1961

forget only at our peril that "power is a trust, conferred on the condition of its just exercise".

These meditations have drawn inspiration from the German writer and philosopher Goethe's wisdom that "one must from time to time repeat what one believes in, proclaim what one agrees with and what one condemns". The thinker's function, as the American political philosopher Barrows Dunham reminded us, is "to contribute our share to the description of reality, to improve, so far as we may, the modes of getting things chosen and done. This is everybody's guarantee of honour in other people's thoughts. It is the sole true objectivity, namely, a bias in favour of mankind."[7] Also, all inquiry and ruminations of the mind find their ultimate justification in Socrates's profound reminder that "an unexamined life is not worth living". And, all writing, as my friend and one of India's prominent public intellectuals, Gurcharan Das, tells us, "is an autobiographical project of self-fashioning". It defines the writer.

The reflective pieces in the book may also be read as "a rational sizing up of the human situation…" which will hopefully serve a useful purpose by adding meaningfully to a clearer understanding of the realities and possibilities of a nation sworn to democracy. The

---

7. Barrows Dunham, *Man Against Myth*, 1947

message of the book, I believe, will have resonance beyond India, in countries where democracies need to ensure their resilience.

The inadequacies of the book are for me to own, which I do. The writings included in it are best read and understood as a continuum of my thoughts encased in the two earlier books. The submissions on the nation's contemporary political and constitutional narrative are open to challenge. To the challengers, I submit, quoting Socrates again, "Yet, I say what is true, although a thing of which it is hard to persuade you…" At this critical juncture of our democratic evolution, the choices that we make must reflect the lessons of history and our own experiences, lest the nation take a negative turn in its trajectory.

Finally, the book is offered as a humble obeisance to the wisdom of the wise and their contribution to the literature of law, leadership and politics. And literature, a continuing conversation spanning the ages, does not exist in a vacuum. It reflects a deeper understanding of the human condition, concerns of the present and hope in the future.

1

Constitutional Rights, Democracy and Judicial Review: A Case for Balanced Constitutionalism[1]

1. Updated and revised article as published in *Economic and Political Weekly* on 13 April 2019

The vexed question of the boundaries of judicial review in the framework of the constitutional separation of powers resurfaces from time to time in different contexts. This is particularly so after the Kesavananda Bharati judgment in 1973[2] by a Bench of thirteen Supreme Court judges. This landmark decision of the largest-ever Bench of India's highest court propounded the 'Basic Structure' doctrine and declared that certain provisions of the Constitution, including those concerning federalism, parliamentary democracy, secularism, the rule of law, the right to life and judicial review, were beyond the amending power of Parliament. The judgment has withstood the test of time and is regarded by legal scholars as an enduring bulwark against the abuse of legislative and executive power. Several decisions of the Court have affirmed that judicial review is an integral part of the Court's inviolate basic structure. These include

2. Kesavananda Bharati Sripadagalvaru v. State Of Kerala And Anr [(1973) 4 SCC 225]

Indira Nehru Gandhi,[3] Minerva Mills,[4] S.R. Bommai,[5] Common Cause case,[6] M. Nagraj,[7] I.R. Coelho,[8] NJAC case,[9] Shayara Bano,[10] Navtej Singh Johar,[11] Dr. Subhash Kashinath Mahajan,[12] Ritesh Sinha,[13] Keisham Meghachandra Singh,[14] Ashwini Kumar Upadhyay,[15] Amarendra Kumar Pandey,[16] Mohd. Latief Magrey,[17]

3. Indira Nehru Gandhi v. Shri Raj Narain & Anr [1975 SCC On Line SC 521]
4. Minerva Mills Ltd and Ors. v. UOI and Ors. [1980 SC 1789]
5. S.R. Bommai v. UOI [1994 SCC (3) 1]
6. Common Cause, A Registered Society v. Union of India [AIR 1999 SC 2979]
7. M. Nagraj & Others v Union of India & Others [(2006) 8 SCC 212]
8. I.R. Coelho v. State of Tamil Nadu [(2007) 2 SCC 1]
9. Advocates on Record Association v. Union of India (2016) 5 SCC 1
10. Shayara Bano v. UOI [(2017) 9 SCC 1]
11. Navtej Singh Johar & Ors. v. UOI [(2018) 10 SCC 1]
12. Dr. Subhash Kashinath Mahajan v. State of Maharashtra [(2018) 6 SCC 454]
13. Ritesh Sinha v. State of U.P & Anr. [(2019)8 SCC1]
14. Keisham Meghachandra Singh v. The Hon'ble Speaker Manipur Legislative Assembly [2020 SCC OnLine SC55]
15. Ashwini Kumar Upadhyay v. UOI [W.P. Civil No. 943 of 2021]
16. Amarendra Kumar Pandey v. Union of India & Ors. [2022 SC 600]
17. Mohd. Latief Magrey v. UT of J &K [Case No. 6544 of 2022]

Satendra Kumar Antil,[18] Indian Oil Corporation,[19] Macawber Beekay,[20] Anoop Baranwal,[21] et al.

The Court has been repeatedly petitioned to review the constitutionality of several legislative measures, more so after the pronouncement of the Kesavananda Bharati judgment, on various grounds, including on the touchstone of the 'Basic Structure' doctrine. Over the years, the Court's expansive exercise of judicial review jurisdiction has embraced several fields of activity, otherwise considered within the exclusive purview of the executive and the legislative wings of the Indian state. This is because of the nature of public law litigation and a liberal view taken by constitutional courts regarding the standing of citizens to invoke legal remedies in the public interest.

A palpable sense of disquiet in the coordinate branches of the government at the expansion of judicial remit is evident. The vice president's vocal expression of reservation about the Supreme Court's capacious exercise of judicial review of legislative and executive functions has once again ignited a debate about the

18. Satendra Kumar Antil v CBI [2022 OnLine SC 825]

19. The Indian Oil Corporation & Ors. v. Ajit Kumar Singh &Anr. [2023 SC 478]

20. BTL EPC Ltd. v. Macawber Beekay Pvt. Ltd and others [2023 sc 834]

21. Anoop Baranwal v. UOI Ministry of Law & Justice [2023 SCC OnLine SC 216]

Court's role as the chosen arbiter of the constitutional equilibrium of dispersed sovereign power. Reservations by the vice president have been expressed in the context of the Court's decision in the state of Tamil Nadu,[22] concerning the exercise of the governor's discretion in giving assent to legislative Bills. In this case, the Court invalidated the governor's action in withholding assent to the bills passed by the legislative assembly of the state for an unreasonably long time. It held that the conduct of the governor was unconstitutional and that it was permissible for the Court to read into the silences of the Constitution an implicit obligation on the part of the governor to exercise constitutional discretion reasonably and impartially. Relying upon government circulars, the Court held that the decision by the governor and President concerning assent to legislative bills is required to be taken within three months from the date of the receipt of the government's recommendation for assent.

The judgment of the Court is an exceptional essay in judicial scholarship, intellectual integrity and felicity of expression. However, the extension of the Court's logic to the exercise of presidential prerogative under Article 201 of the Constitution and its suggestion to the President to seek the Court's Advisory Opinion when

22. State of Tamil Nadu v. The Governor of Tamil Nadu & Anr. [2025 SC 419 {W.P.(C) No. 1239/2023}]

deciding on bills reserved by the governor has raised questions about judicial overreach.

In an unprecedented move and what is seen as a clear disapproval of the decision, the President has sought the Supreme Court's Advisory Opinion on the key issues decided in the judgment. Pertinently, the Advisory Opinion of the Court by a larger Bench on substantial questions of constitutional law will be non-binding and cannot displace a binding judicial precedent. The request for opinion is, therefore, seen as a possible opening for review of the judgment, should the Advisory Opinion differ from the ratio and reasoning of the Tamil Nadu case. The issues upon which the Advisory Opinion has been sought pertain essentially to the "constitutional boundaries of executive and judicial authority…" The reference also seeks the Court's view on several other questions, including whether "…the judiciary can modify or override constitutional powers exercised by the President or governor through Article 142", which has been interpreted as conferring upon the Supreme Court, judicial power of the widest amplitude to do justice.

The issue regarding the limits of judicial review has assumed an enhanced significance considering the expansion of executive power and the tendency of legislative majorities to push through the majoritarian agendas without adequate deliberation and attention to the perspective of the Opposition. Integral to the debate is a historic distrust of the people in concentrated power and the role of the people's representatives in reflecting the will of the people.

The philosophical foundation of judicial review in constitutional democracies was articulated by Alexander Hamilton in his much-cited view in the *Federalist No. 78*, that the limitations on federal power "can be presumed in practice in no other way than through the medium of courts of justice, whose duty it is to declare all acts contrary to the manifest tenor of the Constitution void..." The Court's power of judicial review is validated essentially on the premise that democracy is not merely the rule of the majority. It is also about the protection of human rights that constitute "substantive democracy" and therefore, its exercise in defence of human rights is not anti-democratic.[23] Judicial review is seen simply as the "implementation of the Court's equal participation in Government" and as an antidote "to the excess of democracy".[24] The criticism of an activist judiciary is sought to be addressed by stressing that constitutional interpretation by courts does not, "by any means, suppose a superiority of the judicial to the legislative power. It only supposes that the power of the

23. Aharon Barak, *The Judge in a Democracy*, Princeton University Press, 2006

24. 'A summary of why we need more Judicial Activism' by Suzanna Sherry, Green Bag, 2d, 499

people is superior to both, and that where the will of the legislature declared in its statutes stands in opposition to that of the people, declared in the Constitution, the Judge ought to be governed by the latter rather than the former…"[25] Justifying its remit, the Supreme Court held in Brajendra Singh Yambem that "judicial review is undertaken by the courts not to tilt at legislative authority, but in discharge of a constitutional duty".[26]

Proponents of a wide judicial review jurisdiction argue that it subserves the rule of law.[27] They reject it as being anti-majoritarian or anti-democratic by locating its sanction in the Constitution itself and the social contract that reflects the will of the people. It has also been suggested that the separation of legislative and judicial space is premised on the sometimes misplaced assumption that the legislature "is responsive to the popular will, is attuned to constitutional values and has greater capacity than the judiciary".[28] The judge, it is argued, is "the bridge between life and law", that judicial

25. Alexander Hamilton, *The Federalist* No. 78, See 'The Democratic Character of Judicial Review' by Eugene Rostow, *Harvard Law Review*, Vol. 66, December 1952 number 2

26. Brajendra Singh Yambem v. Union Of India And Anr [(2016)9 SCC20]

27. A.V. Dicey, *Introduction to the Study of Law and the Constitution*, 10th Edn., Macmillan (1956), pp. 406.

28. David Landau, "Political Institutions and Judicial Role in Comparative Constitutional Law", 51 *Harvard International Journal* 319 (320) as cited in Rehan Abeyratne, "Socio-Economic Rights in the Indian Constitution: Towards a Broader Conception of Legitimacy", 39 *Brook. J. Int'l L.* (214), at pp. 58.

adjudication actualises the Constitution and is an "inescapable tremor in the landscape of constitutional jurisprudence".[29]

It is asserted that "... the Constitution functions as a basis and framework of legitimate power. Subjection of rulers to the condition laid down by the people is the explicit function of the Constitution..." And that "the root idea of the Constitution is that man can be free because the State is not".[30]

Another generally acknowledged justification for judicial review is that it advances the cause of justice, human rights, reasonableness, tolerance, and the basic principles of morality and good faith, all of which constitute the substantive aspect of democracy. And those choices that are ex facie unreasonable and inconsistent with democracy[31] are invalidated in a judicial review exercise. Human rights, it is suggested, are an ethical force to provide "inspiration for legislation" and "are strong ethical pronouncements as to what should be

29. Bingham, *The Business of Judging*, Oxford University Press," (2000), pp. 195.

30. See Supra Note 32.

31. Aharon Barak, *The Judge in a Democracy*, Princeton University Press (2006), p.33; Ronald Dworkin, *Law's Empire*, Harvard University Press (1988), p. 356.

done…"[32] These arguments account for the role of the judiciary as a political and policy-making institution.[33]

It is argued that "…power may justly be compared to a great river, which, kept within its bounds, is both beautiful and useful but when it overflows its banks, it is then too impetuous to be stemmed, it bears down all before it brings destruction and devastation wherever it comes…"[34] Leo Strauss's reminder of Socrates's condemnation to death by Athenian democracy is recalled to argue that liberal democracy needs to protect itself against "the rule of the mob".[35] James Madison's felicity resonates as the inspiring clincher of the justification of judicial review: "In framing a government which is to be administered by men over men," argued Madison, "the great difficulty lies in this: You must first enable the government to control the governed and in the next place oblige it to control itself. A dependence on the people is no doubt the primary control on the government, but experience has taught

32. Amartya Sen, *The Idea of Justice*, Penguin Allen Lane (2009), p. 363.

33. Upendra Baxi, *The Indian Supreme Court and Politics*, Eastern Book Company (1979), pp.10-30.

34. Andrew Hamilton, "The Cause of Liberty" (4 August 1735) cited in *The Penguin Book of Historic Speeches*, edited by Brain MacArthur, Penguin, (2012), p. 67.

35. Leo Strauss, *Liberalism, Ancient and Modern* (Chicago and London): The University of Chicago Press (1968).

mankind the necessity of auxiliary protections."[36] Edmund Burke famously articulated the rationale of judicial review. "It is in the nature of despotism," he warned, "to abhor power held by any means but its own momentary pleasure; and to annihilate any intermediate solution between boundless strength on its part and total debility on the part of the people."[37] John Adams expressed a similar sentiment stating that "despotism or unlimited sovereignty or absolute power is the same in a majority of a popular assembly, an aristocratic council, an oligarchical junto, and a single emperor…"[38]

"The judgment of the voter is not a substitute for the judgment of the law," argued Judge Aharon Barak in his dissenting Opinion in a case of corruption and fraud brought before the Supreme Court of Israel.[39] The Constituent Assembly debates that led to the framing of our Constitution suggest a clear disapproval of the concentration of authority, in favour of dispersed and accountable power through institutional balances.

It is in this framework of history and philosophy of limited government that the rationale of judicial review

---

36. See: Madison in: James Madison, Alexander Hamilton, John Jay, *The Federalist Papers*, edited by Isaac Kramnick, Penguin Books (1987), pp. 319-320.

37. Joao Carlos Espada, *The Anglo-American Tradition of Liberty: A View from Europe*, Routledge (2016), p. 164.

38. Letter to Thomas Jefferson, 13 November 1815

39. Amitai – Citizens for Proper Administration and Integrity v. Prime Minister of Israel, 47 (5) P.D.441; See: Supra Note 49, pp. 242-243.

has been repeatedly reiterated by the Supreme Court. Thus, in I.R. Coelho,[40] the Court, referring to Articles 14, 19, and 21, articulated judicial review as "…the principles of constitutionality … apart from the rule of law and separation of powers…" reasoning that "the principle of constitutionalism is now a legal principle which requires control over the exercise of government power…"[41]

However, the indisputable logic of judicial review thus articulated cannot discount the compelling case cautioning judicial restraint. It is contended that in a democracy, people exercise their sovereignty through elected representatives and not through the unelected judges who must defer to the wisdom of parliamentary majorities. "Judicial supremacy," "judicial excessivism", and "despotism of an oligarchy" are seen as antithetical to democracy[42] and contrary to its first principles. It is contended that the unfettered power of judicial review negates the core of the democratic principle, viz., that ultimate sovereignty vests in the people and is exercised through their elected representatives. Thus, arrangements of governance embodied in the Constitution resulting from the exercise of the free will

40. I R Coelho v State of Tamil Nadu (2007) 2 SCC 1

41. Ibid. p. 79, para 43

42. Scott M. Noveck, "Is Judicial Review Compatible with Democracy," 6 (2), Cardozo Pub. L. Pol'y & Ethics J. 2008, at p. 401; Also, Jeremy Waldron, "The Core of the Case Against Judicial Review", 115 Yale L.J. 1346 (2006).

of the people cannot be used to deprive the sovereign masters of the right of final decision over their destiny. It is argued that "juridification of politics politicisation of the judiciary"[43] would be a loss for both the legislature and judiciary, and that the judiciary cannot act as a "censor of all governmental action". The essence of the philosophy of civil government flowing from the will of the people, as propounded by John Locke, retains its appeal.[44] Activism of the Court in a vast expansion of the judicial review function has been criticised also on the basis of "institutional competence"[45] and for running the risk of taking on a policy role "to a degree characteristic of political authority and being mistaken for one".[46] It is suggested that "most dangerous is the power given to judges to find their own direction, a

---

43. D.P. Currie, *The Constitution of the Federal Republic of Germany*, University of Chicago Press (1994), p. 319.

44. John Locke, *The Second Treatise on Civil Government*, (1690), Prometheus Books (1986), Amherst, New York: "…If a controversy arise betwixt a prince and some of the people in a matter where the law is silent or doubtful, and the thing be of great consequence, I should think the proper umpire in such a case should be the body of the people (who at first lodged that trust in him) how far they meant it should extend? … The power that every individual gave the society when he entered into it can never revert to the individuals again, as long as the society lasts, but will always remain in the community…"

45. See: Sandra Fredman, "*Allies or Subversives: The Judiciary and Democracy,*" Is. L.R., Vol.32, at pp. 407-447. Also, T.R.S. Allan, *Deference, Defiance and Doctrine: Defining the Limits of Judicial Review*, (2010) 60 University of Toronto L.J., at p. 55: "Judges alone cannot claim to be more faithful to the general moral commitments of the legal order…"

46. Per Pathak J., in Bandhua Mukti Morcha v Union of India, (1984) 3 SCC 161; Also see, Balco Employees Union v Union of India, (2002) 2 SCC 336.

power for which they have neither the competence nor the legitimacy..."[47]

"Without the comforting cloak of parliamentary intent, what democratic credentials can judges claim for judicial lawmaking..."[48] is a much-asked question. The finality of judicial wisdom is also questioned, as is "abusive constitutionalism"[49] and "autocratic legalism".[50] It is asserted that the Supreme Court cannot rewrite the Constitution through interpretation, nor can the judiciary "misperceive" its institutional function of protecting constitutional rights as an "unchallenged lord in a feudal society" (The *Hindu*, 27 August 2025)

In an eloquent exposition in the NJAC case,[51] Justice Chelameswar, in his minority judgment, rejected a distrust of the legislators in securing the constitutional fundamentals and argued that:

518. ...to assume or assert that the judiciary alone is concerned with the preservation of liberties and does that job well, is an assumption that is dogmatic, bereft of evidentiary basis and historically disproved...

47. See Supra Note 52, p. 447

48. See Supra Note 52, at p. 428.

49. David E Landau, "Abusive Constitutionalism", 47 *Davis L Review* 189 [2013]

50. Kim Lane Scheppele, "Autocratic Legalism", 85 *U.Chi. L. Review* 545 [2018]

51. Advocates on Record Association v. Union of India (2016) 5 SCC 1

519. Our experience is not dissimilar. Judgments in A.K. Gopalan v. State of Madras (AIR 1950 SC 27), Union of India v. Sankalchand Himatlal Sheth & Anr (1977) (4) SCC 193, ADM Jabalpur v. S. Shukla etc. (AIR 1976 SC 1207) (to mention a few) should lead to an identical inference that in difficult times when political branches cannot be counted upon, neither can the judiciary. The point sought to be highlighted is that the judiciary is not the only constitutional organ which protects liberties of the people…

A decision of the Apex Court, which invoked "essentiality" to test the freedom of religion, has been criticised as an "obscure exercise that draws the court into an area which is arguably beyond its competence and gives power to judges to decide on matters of religion. In a way, the Court takes over the clergy… "[52] The majority decision of the Court in Abhiram Singh v. C.D. Commachen (Dead) By LRs,[53] seeking to expansively define the scope of Section 123 of the Representation of the People Act that prohibits appeals to religion, caste, etc., in elections, has been questioned as an example of "high moral principle but dubious law". Questioning the expansion of judicial power, it has

52. Faizan Mustafa, "The Supreme Court Shouldn't Act As Clergy", *Hindustan Times*, 16 December 2016, at p. 16.

53. (2017) 2 SCC 629.

been argued that democracy cannot "look for survivors outside the democratic process".[54] Cardozo's caution is eloquent. "There is no assurance," he wrote, "that the rule of majority will be the expression of perfect reason when embodied in the Constitution or in statute. We ought not to expect more of it when embodied in the judgment of the Courts…"[55] Nor can we disregard his celebrated wisdom that "…the great tides and currents which engulf the rest of men do not turn aside in their course and pass the judges by…'[56]

Judicial infallibility has been disclaimed by the Court itself.[57] Ely, while supporting limited judicial review as a "platonic" guardian of democracy, suggests that "…it is entirely incompatible with democracy for courts to define their mission as one of correcting elected officials

54. Pratap Bhanu Mehta, "High Principle, Dubious Law", Indian Express, 4 January 2017, available at <http://indianexpress.com/article/opinion/col mns/supreme-court-hindutva-case-representation-people-act-rpa 4457663/>(last accessed November, 2019). Also, per James Bradley Thayer, "…the court can only disregard the Act [of legislature] where those who have the right to make laws have not merely made a mistake but have made a very clear one – so clear that it is not open to rational argument…", 7 *Harvard Law Review*, at p.144 as cited in John Hart Ely, *On Constitutional Ground*, Princeton University Press, 1996, at p. 8.

55. Benjamin N. Cardozo, *The Nature of the Judicial Process*, Universal Law Publishing Co., (2008 Reprint).

56. Ibid. at p. 168

57. Per Pathak J. in Bandhua Mukti Morcha v Union of India, (1984) 3 SCC 161: "…And we must remember that we wear the mantle of infallibility only because our decisions are final."; Also, Per Justice Jackson in Brown v. Allen: 344 US 443 (1953): "We are not final because we are infallible, but we are infallible only because we are final."

who have strayed too far either from what the judges think is right or from what they claim they know (and the legislators do not) that the people really think is right… "[58] The burgeoning judicial power has been criticised as "…little more than an incantation and vehicle for judicial ideologies to masquerade as constitutional evolution…" and "…academicians substituting an ideal of justice for the concrete articulation of justice actually in the Constitution…"[59] Even those supportive of an expansive review jurisdiction have suggested that "judicial review is inherently adapted to preserving broad and flexible lines of constitutional growth, not to operating as a continuously active factor in legislative or executive decisions".[60]

Fuelled by a global decline of democracies, witnessed in the perceptible loosening of constraints on the exercise of legislative and executive power, amid concerns at the same time about the expanding judicial reach, pertinent questions about the scope of judicial review have taken centre stage in the politico-constitutional discourse.

58. John Hart Ely, *On Constitutional Ground*, Princeton University Press (1996)

59. Gautam Bhatia, *The Transformative Constitution*, Harper Collins India (2019), at pp. xxxix and xxxiv.

60. See Supra Note 61, p. 198.

These include the following:

- Can the original justification for the Court's anti-majoritarian role be used to equate supremacy of the Constitution and judicial independence with "judicial supremacy"? Does the Indian Constitution envisage for the judges the role of "republican school masters"?[61]
- Can judicial review be a means to "energise the moral order",[62] considering that "courts cannot declare a limitation or constitutional requirement under the notion of having discovered some ideal norm…"?[63]
- Assuming a decline of the democratic order, can the judiciary act as "chemotherapy for a carcinogenic body politics", as suggested by Professor Upendra Baxi?[64] Can the Court become "co-governor of the nation", reading the Constitution as an open-ended text, providing it with new powers to invent

---

61. Ralph Lerner, "The Supreme Court as Republican School Master", S.Ct. Rev. (1967), at pp. 127-80, cited in Pratap Bhanu Mehta, "The Rise of Judicial Sovereignty", *J. Democr.*, 18 (2) (2007), at pp. 70-83.

62. Jerome A. Barron, "The Ambiguity of Judicial Review: A Response to Prof. Bickel", *Duke L.J.* (1970), at pp. 591-604.

63. Ibid at p. 510.

64. Upendra Baxi, Introduction to S. P. Sathe, *Judicial Activism in India*, Oxford University Press (2001), p. 3 as cited in Pratap Bhanu Mehta, "The Rise of Judicial Sovereignty", *J. Democr.* 18 (2) (2007), at pp. 70-83.

new rights? Can courts be allowed to second-guess the legislative values or moral judgments?[65]

- Does an expansive judicial review jurisdiction that promotes judicial veto over legislation decrease the autonomy of the individual and, in the process, negate democracy itself?
- Where does one locate the "equilibrium between the Scylla of insensitive detachment suggesting indifference and the Charybdis of unwarranted intrusion…"[66] to fix the frontiers of constitutionally dispersed power?

It is submitted that the Court's jurisdiction as "sentinel on the qui vive" for protection and advancement of fundamental rights merits loud affirmation on first principles of constitutionalism. But in the articulation of constitutional fundamentals, the Court ought not to be seen as dismissive or disdainful of the processes of democratic governance. It may wish to ask itself "… whether and for how long, the people will maintain their confidence in a court that has lost its confidence

65. Lon L. Fuller, *The Morality of Law*, Yale University Press (1969), p. 54: "…We cannot neatly distinguish between what Parliament has done and what we think it ought morally to do…"

66. G.L. Peiris, "Public Interest Litigation in the Indian Subcontinent: Current Dimensions", 40 (1) *Int'l & Comp. L.Q.*, at pp. 66-90, at p. 89.

in them and in their leaders…"[67] Lok Sabha debates indicate "…Parliament's role to offer competing interpretation of the Constitution…", and record the views of parliamentarians that "…the Indian Parliament did not conceive of the Supreme Court and High Courts as being the exclusive or final interpreters of constitutional rights…"[68] Judicial Review cannot be nor is intended to be a substitute for democratic policy making based on political contestation through the processes of democracy.

The primacy of Parliament as reflecting the will of the people is implicit in the design of the Constitution and is, therefore, not inconsistent with constitutional supremacy. The presumption that the legislature understands the needs of its people and that even its discrimination and classifications are based on adequate grounds has been acknowledged by the Supreme Court itself.[69]

---

67. Kenneth Harle, Montgomery Pamela S. Karlan, "Democracy and Disdain", 126 *Harv. L. Rev.* 1 (2012).

68. Excerpts from Nehru's Lok Sabha Speech in 1951 suggesting that Members of Parliament reflected the "real intention" of the framers of the Constitution and "…have a good general broad idea of what we intended…" is apposite; See: Chintan Chandrachud, *Balanced Constitutionalism*, Oxford University Press (2017), pp. 108-115.

69. In Re: Special Reference, Supra Note 1; State of Kerala v M.N. Thomas, AIR 1976 SC 490; Ibid. at p. 127

Pascal's spirit of "self-search and self-reproach", referred to by Cardozo[70] and reflected in several judgments of the Court, will sustain over time the otherwise wide ambit of judicial review. The Court can, thus, "be a light unto the nations" even if it cannot be a "sheriff unto the nations".[71] Justice Frankfurter's wisdom articulated in his dissenting judgment in Trop v. Dulles,[72] makes the point: "…Judicial power," he declared, "is not immune against human weakness … it must observe a fastidious regard for limitation on its own power and this precludes the Court's giving effect to its own notions of what is wise or politic … Self-restraint is of the essence of judicial oath…" While reiterating that "…abnegation in a matter where power is conferred to protect the interests of others against measures which are violative of the Constitution is fraught with serious consequences…"[73] the Supreme Court has affirmed that "…restraint stabilises the judiciary in a system of inter-branch equality…"[74]

70. Ibid p. 172.

71. Justice José A. Cabranes, "Withholding Judgment: Why U.S. Courts Shouldn't Make Foreign Policy", *Foreign Affairs*, September/October 2015, at pp. 125-133 (adapted from the 2015 Leslie H. Arps Memorial Lecture, which was delivered at the New York City Bar Association).

72. Trop v Dulles (1958) 356 US 86 as cited in (2008) 3 SCC 221, pp. 227-228.

73. Khanna, J. in State of Madras v. Khanchand, (1974) 1 SCC 549, cited with approval in Shayara Bano v Union of India, (2017) 9 SCC 1, pp. 89-90.

74. Per A.K. Mathew and Markandey Katju JJ in Divisional Manager, Aravalli Golf Club v Chander Hass, 2008 1 SCC 683.

The logic of a balanced exercise of judicial power as an assurance of institutional stability is inbuilt in the constitutional structure. Evidently, interpretative finality vested in the Supreme Court cannot be used to conflate constitutional supremacy with judicial supremacy. The imperative of a restrained exercise of constituent power is inherent in the definition of bounded power and reinforced by a presumption of constitutionality of legislation. Without being constrained by apprehensions of institutional conflict in a compelling case requiring interference, the Court is expected to guard against a debilitating inter-institutional conflict. Clearly, what is required is a vocabulary of constitutional discourse that navigates the extremes of "judicial submission" and "judicial despotism", remembering that in a democracy, the three branches cannot be adversaries and that they are all in the justice business, together.[75]

Judicial intervention in policy choices of the government/Parliament has raised troubling questions about the constitutional balance of power. Decisions of the Court relating to constitutional amendments approved by Parliament by more than the requisite

75. Beverly McLachlin, "Charter Myths", 33 U.B.C. Law Review 23, 31 (1999); And "Courts and legislators are … joint and supplementary rather than alternative exclusive protectors and promoter of rights…", Stephen Gardbaum, *The New Commonwealth Model of Constitutionalism: Theory and Practice*, Cambridge University Press, (2013).

majority in the NJAC matter[76] and the Election Commissioners case,[77] as also some aspects of its judgment in the Tamil Nadu case, could be critiqued as an unwarranted intrusion in the legislative domain. The highest Court is generally expected to uphold the constitutionality of legislative and administrative policy decisions on the well-settled principle of presumption of constitutionality, unless palpably arbitrary.

This does not, however, interdict the Court from censuring legislative indifference or absolutism and the excesses of the executive branch where necessary, in a solemn reminder of its role as an "auxiliary protection" against the arbitrary exercise of power. Indeed, the judicially discovered limitation on Parliament's legislative powers in cases concerning "fundamental substantive values and political processes that suppress voice or systematically discriminate against minorities" is a legitimate function of constitutional courts. The judicious exercise of its review function has received popular approval over the years and has added to the Court's prestige.

The difficulty, however, is the absence of consistency and a subjective exercise of the review jurisdiction, ranging from judicial abdication to interpretative overreach. How else can one understand the

76. Advocates on Record Association v. Union of India (2016) 5 SCC 1.

77. Anoop Baranwal v. UOI Ministry of Law & Justice, (2023) SCC Online.

constitutional Court's ambivalence in granting bail in several deserving cases, although this trend has been fortunately reversed in recent times, and its refusal to even nudge the government for enacting an anti-custodial torture legislation, while recommending one against mob lynching. Likewise, while recognising the limits of its review function in several cases, it has chosen to strike down even constitutional amendments proposed by the executive to effectuate key policy choices.

Evidently, egregious wrongs related to policy and political choices of a democratic government can finally be addressed in the court of the people alone, a view that finds support in constitutional philosophy. Indeed, "...the people are well aware that their own political exertions and not the long arm of the Supreme Court, must be their chief reliance in moulding the body of regulatory legislation to their heart's desire".[78] The need to resist the temptation of supplanting the legislative judgment with that of the Court, unless clearly arbitrary, ought to be resisted to ensure a harmonious functionality of dispersed constitutional power.

In the Indian context, the doctrine of "Basic Structure" as a judicially discovered limitation on legislative power is entitled to deference, consistent

78. See Supra Note 82.

with the Court's ordained role. And yet, it is necessary to ensure against a sweeping interpretative expansion of constitutional fetters on the legislative and executive functions to ensure a moderated exercise of judicial power that accords with the moral, social and political sentiments of the nation.

In a functional democracy, people, speaking through their representatives, cannot be denied the right to reframe and review their constitutional tenets in the light of wisdom born of experience, as long as the purity of electoral processes to ascertain the true will of the people can be ensured through a credible and uncorrupted democratic process. To suggest, even by implication, that the framers of a democratic Constitution intended to deny the people's representatives the right to revisit the Constitution for all times on an assumption of finality of the stated popular will, regardless of the context and the transformative socio-political changes, will be a negation of the history and essence of evolving constitutionalism.

Thus, legislative jurisdiction in a democracy admits essentially of only such fetters as are necessary to preserve the fundamental and natural rights of the people, prevent the exercise of oppressive State power and ensure the purity of electoral processes to guard against a situation where "democratic governance is effectively converted from a multi-to single player enterprise".[79] The decision of the Court, therefore, to entertain the Opposition parties' challenge to the Special Intensive Revision (SIR-2025) of the Bihar Electoral Rolls that could allegedly result in denying hundreds of thousands of people their voting rights was an entirely legitimate exercise of the power of judicial review. Beyond the aforestated limits on legislative and executive power, the judgment of the people's representatives on policy choices merits deference. Abraham Lincoln's caution sounded in his inaugural address is eloquent. "If the policy of the Government on vital questions affecting the whole people," said the President, "is to be irrevocably fixed by decision of the Supreme Court, then the people will have ceased to be their own rulers, having practically resigned their government into the hands of that eminent Tribunal."[80] Justice Stone's "sober second thought" description of judicial review conveys the limitations of the reviewing function.

An embrace of the "passive virtues" of judicial restraint[81] will ensure the longevity of judicial review conceived as a bulwark against authoritarianism. The

---

79. Stephen Gardbaum, p.1439.

80. Brutus, 1788.

81. A. Bickel, *The Least Dangerous Branch* [1962], C. Black, pp. 27-33,68-72, ch. 4 cited in R.L. Brilmayer, "Judicial Review, Justiciability and the Limits of the Common Law Method" in *Boston University Law Journal*, Vol 57, p.807 at 818.

necessity of self-imposed restraint on the exercise of judicial power has been reiterated by the Court in the Tamil Nadu case also, holding that [in] "the exercise of self-imposed restraint ... courts do not venture into areas of governance in which the Constitution gives a prerogative solely to the executive".[82] Justice Sonia Sotomayor's powerful dissent in the Texas Abortion case[83] underscored the necessity of judicial restraint, drawing a distinction between the "raw exercise of judicial power" and judicial review.

Chief Justice B.R. Gavai, in his address at the Oxford Union, is reported to have endorsed a balanced exercise of judicial review jurisdiction. The Chief Justice has stated that "Judicial activism is here to stay. At the same time, judicial activism should not be turned into judicial terrorism." In a similar vein, Justice Surya Kant, in his inaugural address at the Envision India Conclave in San Francisco, has reportedly stated that "true constitutional guardianship lies not in dominance but in restraint—an ethos that reaffirms the judiciary's legitimacy in a vibrant democracy ... Courts mustn't supplant the role of the legislature or override the will of the people. Instead, they must act as facilitators of democratic dialogue—strengthening participatory governance, protecting the vulnerable and ensuring that the rule of

---

82. See Supra Note 29, para 418, p. 337.

83. United States v. Texas, 595 U.S. (2021).

law prevails even in moments of political uncertainty … Judicial overreach risks unsettling the delicate balance of power."[84] The two senior-most judges of the Supreme Court have thus clearly indicated that judicial review, as an integral component of the basic structure doctrine, has to be harmonised with the other core features of the Constitution. Implicit in their studied statements is an admission of judicial overreach from time to time. The timely reminder from the distinguished judges will serve to strengthen the Court's remit as the judicial arbiter of constitutional conscience.

Clearly, a moderated exercise of judicial power will obviate the debilitating inter-institutional confrontation and reinforce democratic constitutionalism. Pertinently, judicial review as a countervailing constitutional arrangement has been sustained by majoritarian support because of the popular faith in the integrity of the Court in drawing the limits of its own power and because judicial review also serves to legitimise majoritarian policy choices.[85] Fidelity to the constitutional equilibrium and search for the "intermediate" is thus of the essence when drawing the contours of judicial review in a democratic polity. The invalidation of the

---

84. The *Times of India*, 12 June 2025.

85. James R. Rogers and Joseph Daniel Ura, "A Majoritarian Basis for Judicial Countermajoritarianism", in *Journal of Theoretical Politics*, Vol 32(3), pp. 435-459.

Constitution amendment in the NJAC case[86] and its decision in the Election Commissioners Appointments case[87] are, in the writer's respectful submission, illustrative of the Court's impermissible intrusions in the legislative domain and dismissive of the considered policy preferences of parliamentarians, particularly, in matters involving constitutional amendments by special legislative majorities. The proffered justification for the judgments is that these are in aid of securing judicial independence, indisputably, a part of the basic structure of the Constitution. However, the equivalence sought to be established between the mode and manner of judicial appointments through the extant appointments mechanism and judicial independence is stretched, considering that the highest judicial appointments solely by the government in the past have not been faulted for their lack of independence in the discharge of judicial functions.

And, despite its internal coherence and unexceptionable constitutional logic anchored in the requirement of reasonability in the exercise of constitutional power, the judgment of the Court in the Tamil Nadu case can be questioned for its directions (cloaked as a suggestion) to the President to seek its advice under Article 143 of the Constitution on legal issues concerning the legality

86. Advocates on Record Association v. Union of India (2016) 5 SCC 1

87. Anoop Baranwal v. UOI Ministry of Law & Justice, (2023) SCC On Line

of legislative Bills requiring Presidential assent. This has been argued, not unreasonably, as an unwarranted judicial advice in the matter of the exercise of sovereign discretion, not necessitated by the scope of the legal challenge before the court that was limited essentially to the conduct of the governor of Tamil Nadu. This part of the judgment can also be faulted in view of the prescribed processes, including those pertaining to legal counsel available to the President for decision-making in the exercise of sovereign functions, as argued elsewhere in the book.

The undue delay in hearing several cases of substantial public interest involving large-scale infraction of human rights has contributed to doubts about the Court's internal mechanisms, adversely impacting its prestige as the arbiter of constitutional morality. It has been argued that "a Court that can assemble a bench overnight to decide the fate of dogs but cannot summon the will to hear bail pleas pending for two years undermines its own moral authority". (Saurav Das's *#NewColumn* referring to activist Surendra Gadling's bail application).

Also, as an institutional instrument to tame executive power and legislative majorities to the discipline of the Constitution, it is necessary for the Court to ensure the implementation of its edicts, so that these do not remain mere statements of pious intent. The fact that some of the Court's important decisions have remained substantially unimplemented has weakened the Court's review jurisdiction. And, the much-criticised oral observations by the judges during the course of hearings suggesting unwarranted subjective and moral judgments, have done much damage to the prestige of the Court. Scathing remarks from the Bench against judges whose judgment is appealed in the Apex Court as in a recent case of a judge of the Allahabad High Court or a wholly injudicious suggestion by the Court to the Leader of the Opposition in the Lok Sabha as to what to say and from which forum to exercise his right of expression, obliquely questioning the political leader's nationalism, is a wholly unacceptable judicial transgression. Such self-inflicted injuries have dented the Court's prestige and the exercise of its judicial review jurisdiction.

Conceived as the people's instrument against the exercise of oppressive majoritarian power, judicial review cannot itself become oppressive or be seen as pitted against the people themselves as distinguished from the mob or manipulated legislative majorities. Its life and undoubted utility depend on the moral and judicial correctness of its exercise, which ought not to be seen as an interpretative encroachment of the functions entrusted to the coordinate wings of a democratic state, a view premised upon the resilience of the nation's democratic processes to self-correct the glaring infractions of the republic's fundamentals.

Judges, wisened by experience, disciplined by law and elevated by knowledge, are expected to weigh and balance competing values and principles, a function central to their role. We know that power has reasoned in every age, and it is in the wisdom of the wise that enduring answers to some of the most profound questions of our time will be found. The challenge is to find the wisest and bravest amongst us to nurture and invigorate the institutions designed to serve the ideals of the republic.[88]

88. Since this essay on the scope of constitutional judicial review is written in the Indian context, reference to "Court" in the book denotes the Supreme Court of India, but the principles enunciated with reference to the boundaries of judicial review are applicable to constitutional democracies that have invested their courts with the reviewing power. Appendices II and III contain expressions of the author's views on the subject in interviews.

2

Let Justice Prevail Over Power[1]

Should the principles of legal due process in the discovery of truth be compromised to win the political battle of perception, in a trade-off between political expediency and constitutional principles?

1. The *Punjabi Tribune*,7 May 2025; The *Tribune*, 9 May 2025

Charge-sheeting of the Gandhis and others by the Enforcement Directorate (ED) in the National Herald case for alleged money laundering and criminal misappropriation of public property has invited countrywide protests by the Congress and its sympathisers. They see the criminal case as one without a basis in fact or in law and as a brazen act of political vendetta. The protest by the principal Opposition party has elicited a counter-response by the ruling dispensation.

Speaking through its former law minister, Ravi Shankar Prasad, at a special press conference, the BJP alleged that the accused had misappropriated public property through devious devices and were now seeking to intimidate the Enforcement Directorate. Embarking upon an elaboration of the prosecution's case on the basis of selective leaks, the former minister queried, "If public property worth thousands of crores is misappropriated, why are you protesting and calling it vendetta?" The BJP spokesperson is also reported to have said that no one had a "license to loot". Another cabinet minister in office asserted emphatically, "...it is an open-and-shut case of fraud, corruption, and money laundering."

Clearly, the accused have been condemned by the media, without trial and an opportunity of being heard at the time of cognizance of the charge-sheet, even as the Special Judge trying the case has held that "the right to be heard at any stage of the proceedings breathes life into a fair trial". The usurpation of judicial function by the government's spokespersons to conclude at the inception of the trial itself that the accused had misappropriated property worth thousands of crores offends against the first principles of liberal democracy and constitutional justice.

Such assertions by senior representatives of the government against political adversaries facing criminal charges have fuelled an unrelenting trial of the accused in the print, electronic and social media. This could interfere with the course of justice in several ways. Repeated claims by the BJP of cheating, fraud, misappropriation and money laundering by the accused, when the trial is in its initial stages, could create a hostile public perception against them and influence the judgment of those charged with conducting a judicial trial. Extensive discussion in the media of selective parts from the prosecution complaint, of which judicial cognizance is yet to be taken and for which the case has been adjourned, can cause presumptive prejudice to the accused. This is proscribed in several judgments of the highest court. [Sahara, 2013 and Manu Sharma, 2010], etc. In Manu Sharma's case,[2] the Supreme Court declared that the "...presumption of innocence of an accused is a legal presumption and should not be destroyed at the very threshold through the process of media trial..." And the Constitution Bench in Sahara[3] has ruled that "the presumption of open justice has to be balanced with the presumption of innocence which is now recognised as a human right..."

The accusatory tone and tenor of senior members of the ruling party in their media interaction concerning the case impairs the fundamental right of the accused to a fair trial and presumed innocence, apart from violating their sacrosanct right to reputation, privacy and dignity.

---

2. The Manu Sharma case, popularly known as the Jessica Lal murder case, stirred significant public and media attention. The case involved the murder of Jessica Lal, a model who was bartending at an upscale party in Delhi on the night of 29 April 1999. She was shot dead by Manu Sharma. In April 2010, the Supreme Court of India upheld the Delhi High Court's decision in State v. Manu Sharma, confirming the life sentence. The Court also commented on the broader implications of media influence, noting that media trials cannot dictate outcomes and that judicial decisions must be based solely on admissible evidence.

3. The Sahara India Real Estate Corporation Ltd v. SEBI (2012) case is a landmark judgment delivered by a Constitution Bench of the Supreme Court of India that dealt with the tension between freedom of the press and the right to a fair trial. The case arose when Sahara, involved in ongoing legal proceedings related to alleged financial violations, approached the Court seeking protection from what it claimed was prejudicial media reporting. The Court held that while the principle of open justice is fundamental to a transparent judicial system, it must be balanced against the need for a fair trial, particularly when media coverage risks influencing public perception and judicial outcomes before evidence is properly tested.

Restraint in condemning leaders of political parties without a judicial finding of criminal culpability would ensure that political parties, the lifeblood of democracy, and their leaders are not discredited without a trial in accordance with law [Article 21]. This would afford minimal protection to all political parties against the retributive inclinations of those in power and enhance the quality of democratic engagement.

Lest our democracy be wasted and weakened from within and the nation's founding ideals allowed to wither, the National Herald case should be a test of the republic's adherence to the ideal of equal justice for all. This case will test the inviolability of procedural justice, the integrity of the judicial process and the constitutional promise of justice through fair trial, as against trial by accusation. Media trials, especially in criminal cases, can adversely impact the liberty and freedom of individuals, a result that signals the "soulful requiem to liberty", as Justice D.Y. Chandrachud reminded us in his eloquent dissent in the Bhima Koregaon case.

The National Herald case raises several questions of seminal importance. In an age where "gossip is gospel", must the accused be condemned in the public sphere before a definitive judicial finding of guilt? Can unrestrained public conversations with the media in cases of unproven criminal culpability of individuals be allowed to violate their right to justice and dignity?

Should the principles of legal due process for the discovery of truth in criminal trials be compromised to win the political battle of perception, in a trade-off between political expediency and the constitutional principle? What is the recourse, if any, for those who are punished by the oppressive processes of our criminal justice system and the endless trials that crush the accused before the pronouncement of guilt?

These questions must stay alive in the consciousness of the nation and spur us to civilise ourselves in the use of power. Only then can we redeem the constitutional promise of a just society in which justice is not at the sufferance of the powers that be. The qualitative distinction of the democratic way is the taming of power to the community's sense of fairness and justice. The sanctity of legal processes depends likewise on ensuring that the rigours of law do not result in the miscarriage of justice. Because events shape and define the future, the National Herald case will hopefully be an opportunity to reaffirm the nation's commitment to the rule of law and to draw the boundaries of partisan politics.

3

Innocent Till Guilty

'A civilisation that plays fast and loose with its principles is a dying civilisation.'

–Aimé Césaire

The episode related to Justice Yashwant Varma has raised questions about judicial integrity. However, given the extraordinary nature of the case and gaps in the investigative process, larger questions about the constitutional first principles have taken centre stage.

In his written response dated 22 March to the Chief Justice of Delhi High Court, the judge denied ownership of the cash and claimed that he had no knowledge of how the money found its way to a storeroom in his official residence. He submitted that neither he nor any member of his family had anything to do with the burnt currency notes. He further stated that the storeroom in which the notes were found was easily accessible to members of the staff. Justice Varma also hinted at a possible conspiracy.

Even though the investigation is at a preliminary stage, the judge has been pilloried and condemned. His fundamental rights to privacy and dignity have been violated, and an interim punishment has been imposed upon him without a definitive finding of judicial misconduct. Media trials, repeatedly interdicted by the

Constitutional Courts as violative of the accused's right to fair trial and the rule of law [Sahara India (2012), PUCL (2023)], seem to persist.

The prompt In-House Inquiry initiated by the Chief Justice of India is welcome. However, the withdrawal of judicial work from the judge and his transfer to the Allahabad High Court are punitive and have preceded a finding of judicial misconduct by the Inquiry Committee. This goes against Paragraph 7(ii) of the In-House Inquiry Procedure (1999) against a high court judge. It states that judicial work can be withdrawn from the judge only after a finding of grave judicial misconduct. The unravelling of truth in this case should be consistent with the principles of legal due process and the presumption of innocence—a recognised human right (Sahara), which cannot be compromised to satiate retributive impulses.

The competence of a fact-finding Inquiry Committee to establish the alleged misconduct of Justice Varma to justify harsh punitive consequences in the interim is questionable. Whether the judge can be expected to establish his innocence since, in an action initiated at the highest judicial level, the onus of proving innocence will de facto shift onto him is a pertinent question. Also, will Justice Varma have an effective judicial recourse against a possible adverse finding by the Inquiry Committee appointed by the Chief Justice of India? It is doubtful that the Inquiry Committee will subserve the objective of the in-house procedure of ensuring "a safeguard for the members of the higher judiciary from being maligned or subjected to vilification…", while "making them accountable for their conduct".

The pursuit of truth in the Justice Varma episode should be consistent with the principles of fair administration of justice. This troublesome case should be a moment to coherently reaffirm the Constitution's conception of justice and dignity for all. As the poet and Francophone Aimé Césaire said, "a civilisation that plays fast and loose with its principles is a dying civilisation".

Independent of the merits of this case, a national debate about the advisability of an alternative judicial appointments mechanism has been triggered. Experience underlines the need to redefine judicial independence beyond the exclusive remit of judges to appoint their colleagues. Controversial judicial appointments by the collegium demonstrate that the current system offers no guarantee of the finest lawyers and judges being elevated to the high courts and the Supreme Court. At the same time, it cannot be denied that some of the nation's most eminent judges were appointed when the power of judicial appointments was vested with the Central government. The Supreme Court's striking down of the National Judicial Appointments Commission

(NJAC) as unconstitutional on the premise that its composition ensured the government's dominant say in the appointment of judges is a flawed extension of the doctrine of judicial independence. The highest constitutional court need not be distrustful of the processes of democratic governance and is expected to defer to the policy choices of elected governments based on a broad political consensus. In fact, this principle has been repeatedly affirmed by the apex court itself in several cases. On a larger jurisprudential basis relating to constitutional democracies, the Court may well ask the question asked by the legal scholar Pamela S. Karlan, "…whether and for how long the people will maintain their confidence in a Court that has lost the confidence in them and their leaders…"

It is pertinent to mention that the Inquiry Committee has since submitted its report, based on which the then Chief Justice of India is reported to have recommended impeachment of the judge. Notably, the judge refused to resign despite being advised to do so by the Chief Justice. A bipartisan Impeachment Motion moved in the Lok Sabha on 21 July 2025 has been accepted, and the Lok Sabha Speaker has constituted an Inquiry Committee in accordance with the procedure prescribed. The judicial challenge to the CJI's appointed committee and its findings has since been decisively rejected by the Supreme Court, as was expected.

The views articulated in the piece are asserted.

4

Torture Shadows India's Justice System[1]

Torture in any form is '... a wound in the soul so intangible that there is no way to heal it.'

1. The *Hindu*, 20 March 2025

The ruling by the King's Bench Division of the High Court of Justice in London in the Sanjay Bhandari extradition case (28 February 2025), upholding the fugitive's defence against extradition and proceedings in Tahawwur Rana's Appeal in the United States Supreme Court challenging the latter's extradition are significant judicial developments with larger implications for a constitutional state. Hopefully, these proceedings would spur the government to reinforce India's claim as a professed defender of human rights by enacting a comprehensive law against torture, enabling it to ratify the United Nations Convention against Torture (UNCAT/Convention).

This is because the defence of Bhandari, facing Indian prosecutors for tax evasion and money laundering and of Rana, whose extradition is sought for his role as a conspirator in the 26/11 Mumbai terrorist attack, is premised essentially on credible evidence of endemic custodial torture in India, including India's non-ratification of the Convention. In Bhandari's case, Justices Holroyde and Steyn, while negativing the Indian government's plea for extradition, found that Bhandari faced a real risk of custodial torture in Indian jails and that India had not ratified the UNCAT. Evidence cited by the judges in support of their ruling included the October 2018 Report by the Commonwealth Human Rights Initiative, the UNCAT's 2020 Annual Report on Torture in India, the UN Working Group on Arbitrary Detention [UNWGAD] and the Supreme Court's judgment of 1997 in D.K. Basu.

Rana, in his renewed application for stay of extradition to India, pending decision of his Habeas Corpus Petition, has cited the UK judgment and its reasoning. Other fugitives from Indian law, including Kim Davy, Jagtar Johal, Christian Michel, Mehul Choksi and Nirav Modi, have also challenged the Indian government's extradition request on substantially similar grounds, exposing a legal lacuna that has compromised the effectiveness of the country's criminal justice system.

Failure of the government to ratify the Convention has invited adverse comments at the UN's Universal Periodic Review meetings in view of the government's unkept assurances of ratification. Although one of the earliest Unilateral Declarations against Torture (Resolution number 32/64) was initiated by India in the United Nations General Assembly, and it has ratified several other international treaties against torture, including the Universal Declaration of Human Rights

(1948) and the International Covenant on Civil and Political Rights (1976), the government's ambivalence in ratifying the UNCAT is confounding. Articles 51(c) and 253 of the Constitution mandate respect for international treaties to which India is a party [NALSA (2014), Vishakha (1997)], among others. Regrettably, despite its unreserved commitment to the universally acknowledged right to human dignity, privacy and liberty, India finds itself in the company of discredited non-ratifying dictatorial regimes like Angola, Brunei, Comoros, Gambia, Haiti and Sudan.

Reflecting a broad political consensus on the outlawing of torture based upon deeply felt popular sensitivities, the Select Committee of the Rajya Sabha had recommended a comprehensive anti-torture legislation as early as 2010. The Law Commission recommended likewise in its 273rd Report (2017) and has also furnished a draft of the proposed law for the Government's consideration. The Human Rights Commission of India has similarly supported a standalone domestic law against torture. In an expansive interpretation of Article 21 of the Constitution, the Supreme Court has emphatically declared that torture in any form is an unacceptable infringement of the sacrosanct right to dignity and privacy (D.K. Basu (1997), Puttaswamy (2017), Nambi Narayanan (2018), Romila Thapar (2018). Even so, in Ashwani Kumar (2019), the highest constitutional

Court found itself unable even to nudge the government to consider enacting the requisite law, notwithstanding its several pronouncements suggesting suitable laws on different subjects (Tehseen Poonawalla [2018]; Ranveer Allahbadia [2025], etc.). The Court failed to appreciate that "a lack of legislation may be contrary to the principle of legal certainty", that "it is the function of the Court to provide an effective remedy", and that "it is legitimate for constitutional courts to caution Legislatures against their failure to introduce what they consider as adequate legislation". [Opinion No.18 (2015) Consultative Council of European judges]. Nor did it heed D.Y. Chandrachud's declaration in Jeet S. Bisht (2007), that the doctrine of "'Separation of Powers' allows methods to be used to prod and communicate to an institution either its shortfalls or excesses in discharging its duties…" Even as the Court cautioned in Shayara Bano (2017) that constitutional rights can be defeated through inaction, indifference or ambivalence on the part of other organs of the state, its failure to facilitate the enactment of a comprehensive law against torture is clearly an impermissible abdication of its remit.

In these premises, the extradition cases raise profoundly important and larger questions about a democratic state baulking at fulfilling its compelling constitutional and international obligations. Surely, the price of security cannot be an unconscionable brutalisation of the incarcerated. And whether a democratic state can, by its inaction, demonstrate a brazen disdain for national consensus on a core humanitarian issue is a disconcerting interrogatory. The failure of India over the years to enact a credible anti-torture law indicates the impoverishment of our politics and the indifference of political parties as democratic agents to mediate fundamental policy choices in furtherance of the republic's core values.

Whether or not the cited cases validate Professor Harold Laski's profound insight that "ideas must wait upon events that give them birth", only time will tell. Wiser with the lesson of Guantanamo Bay that torture in state custody irretrievably dents democracy's soft power, the Indian state is expected to vindicate the republic's foundational principles by ratifying the Convention. Clearly, it is time for a nation wedded to democracy and seeking a role as the world's moral arbiter to recognise that a flailing democracy is antithetical to a resurgent Bharat and that torture in any form is "...a wound in the soul so intangible that there is no way to heal it..."[2]

---

2. Tahawwur Rana has since been extradited to India and is currently facing prosecution for his alleged terrorist activities while in custody in India.

5

Signals of Hope from the Supreme Court[1]

Freedom and justice are a product of ennobling politics that prizes liberty and human dignity above all.

1. The *Tribune*, 10 January 2025; *Hindustan Times* (Hindi) 11 January 2025; *Punjabi Tribune* 11 January 2025.

At a time when the nation's fractious political discourse is loaded with conflicting and competing perspectives on constitutionalism, the Supreme Court's role as the arbiter of constitutional conscience assumes heightened significance. Invested with a wide judicial review jurisdiction, the highest constitutional Court has earned the nation's respect for its wisdom in charting the course of balanced constitutionalism in testing times. This is so, notwithstanding the occasional errors of judgment. The Court's acknowledgement of its fallibility and a demonstrated willingness to correct itself has added to its weight as the ultimate forum for judicial justice. In the context of some of its past decisions perceived as equivocal and flawed for want of a clear statement, its recent pronouncements signal a welcome affirmation of liberty and human dignity as the nation's core constitutional values, holding out hope for India's vexed democracy.

Some of the recent decisions that have quietly found their way into the lexicon of human rights jurisprudence and inspire confidence in the resilience of our constitutional institutions deserve mention. These include Surender Panwar (2025), in which the Supreme Court declined to interfere with the observations of the Punjab and Haryana High Court, terming the 14-hour-40-minute-long custodial interrogation of the accused as "not heroic" and "against the dignity of a human being". The decision is a resounding judicial rejection of tortious custodial interrogation, drawing attention to the imperative of fair investigation in accordance with international human rights norms laid down by the United Nations. The decision is particularly significant in the context of India's much delayed ratification of the UN Convention Against Torture (UNCAT), which it had signed in 1997. While the Supreme Court has consistently treated all forms of torture as violative of the individual's right to dignity under Article 21 of the Constitution (D.K. Basu (1997), Tusharbhai Rajnikantbhai Shah (2024) et al.), the Court has been inexplicably ambivalent in nudging the government to legislate a comprehensive legislation against torture in line with the UNCAT as a necessary step towards the elimination of all forms of custodial torture. Having proclaimed the unconstitutionality of investigative measures based on torture, the Court is expected to proactively facilitate the enactment of a comprehensive anti-torture legislation. Its power to do so stems from the willing allegiance of the people to its commands, anchored in legal integrity and reflecting the "community's coherent conception of justice and fairness" (Ronald Dworkin, *Law's Empire*, 1986).

Treading on the libertarian path in a correction of past aberrations and restoring the constitutional balance, the highest Court, speaking through Justices Abhay Oka and A.G. Masih in Athar Parvez (2024), has ruled that the restrictions on bail under a stringent penal statute needed to be harmonised with powers exercisable under the constitutional jurisdiction. It affirmed that long incarceration of the accused without bail is an infraction of Article 21 and that the criminal law doctrine of presumed innocence of the accused is not displaced by the seriousness of the crime with which the accused is charged. The same bench declared in Parvinder Singh Khurana (2024) that a stay of the order granting bail can be passed only rarely and for reasons indicated in the statute. The underlying premise of these judgments is the supremacy of the libertarian philosophy of the Constitution, reaffirmed in Siddhant (2024), in which the Court granted bail to the accused despite stringent statutory conditions. It is hoped that the libertarian judicial approach will soon determine the fate of detenues such as Umar Khalid, who has been in detention since September 2020.

Another significant decision of the Supreme Court in Urmila Dixit (2025), that emphatically asserts the right to dignity and succour for the elderly, merits the nation's fulsome commendation for a compelling moral dimension. Authored by Justice Sanjay Karol, the judgment, in a purposive interpretation of Section 23 of the Maintenance and Welfare of the Parents and Senior Citizens Act, 2007, declared that the "tribunals under the Act may order eviction [of the donee/children] if it is necessary and expedient to ensure the protection of the senior citizen" and can order possession of the property to be transferred if the condition of gift of property is not honoured by the donee. The context is the painful reality of an increasing number of the elderly being neglected, ill-treated and cheated out of their assets and economic security by their children. The decision is a fine example of contextual justice that gives the beneficial legislation its purpose and meaning.

The generative power of the above judgments will doubtless fuel the progressive advancement of constitutional jurisprudence on human rights. But while the nation is entitled to hope that judges will assist in articulating and defining the nation's sense of justice, the burden of ensuring a fair and equitable social order cannot, in fairness, rest with the judiciary alone. Freedom and justice are, in the final analysis, a product of ennobling politics that prizes liberty and human dignity above all. The will of the people, moulded by their shared histories and gathered in a free contestation of ideas, will eventually define the nation's future.

Hopefully, the New Year will herald the beginning of a constructive politics of national renewal inspired by the elevating vision of our founders.

6

A Mandate for Humility[1]

Democratic politics is not morally neutral, and the nation's collective conscience asserts itself eventually.

1. The *Indian Express* 11 October 2024; *Punjabi Tribune* (Punjabi) 22 October 2024.

The results of the elections in Haryana and the Union Territory of Jammu and Kashmir have deservedly invited national attention. The mandate has demonstrated the complexities of democratic politics and underscored the difference between perception and reality. This is certainly true of the Haryana election, about which the general perception, shared by this writer, was that the Congress would reclaim power in the state. However, the results have vindicated the power of the people's collective in scripting their destiny, affirmed the resilience of the democratic spirit and the nation's unswerving commitment to the power of the ballot.

Considering Jammu and Kashmir's troubled history, the peaceful conduct of elections in the Union Territory is a triumph of constitutional democracy and will ensure the emotional integration of Kashmiris with the rest of the country. The wholehearted embracing of the ballot by the people is a defining moment in the deepening of Indian democracy. Given the exceptional political realities of the region and a complex structure of governance within which the National Conference-led government will need to function, constant friction between the people's representatives and constitutional functionaries empowered by the Union government could defeat the gains of democracy and popular aspirations. Omar Abdullah's initial statements hold promise for a constructive dialogue between the two.

The BJP's third consecutive victory in Haryana could have a significant impact on national politics. The largely unexpected victory is a clear indication that after suffering reverses in the Lok Sabha elections, the party applied the correctives and defeated a resurgent Congress through a comprehensive social engineering exercise. Although the election was largely localised, it is futile to deny credit for the victory to Prime Minister Modi, who sanctioned the ouster of his loyalist Manohar Lal Khattar, replacing him with the incumbent chief minister in a caste calculus that dented the anti-BJP sentiment.

The BJP's victory in Haryana signals a weakened bargaining position for the Congress in seat negotiations with its alliance partners in Jharkhand and Maharashtra. The political reverberations of the Haryana election will be felt beyond the state's borders, especially in Punjab, where assembly elections are due in 2027. Bound by a shared history, social affinities and the common challenges of stagnating agricultural economies, the electorate in Punjab and Haryana is influenced by the political mood in their States. The performance of the BJP in Haryana should, therefore, be a matter of concern for Congress, which will try to reclaim power in Punjab in a little over two years from now. While the BJP is certain to increase its vote share in the state, the challenge for the Congress is to offer a refreshing moral and political imagination that can dent the Hindutva narrative whose appeal, with the prime minister as its mascot, remains strong. Despite the stirrings of an anti-incumbency against the AAP government, the party could still get its act together before the elections.

The grand old party of India that hopes to lead a nationwide counter-narrative is expected to present itself as a party with a difference. In its public communication, it should be seen as magnanimous in victory, humble in defeat, tolerant of constructive dissent, respectful of its leaders and partners, and thoughtful in the formulation of policy preferences. It does not speak well of the nation's grand old party to have its spokespersons question the democratic verdict in Haryana. A party that swears by democracy cannot be so overwhelmed by an electoral reverse as to negate a democratic process that gave it nearly 40 per cent vote share and 37 assembly seats. Distributing 'jalebis' without waiting for the result was in poor taste. Must we forget that democratic politics is also about the opponent's dignity, notwithstanding the provocation? Also, the way forward for the Congress is not to look for scapegoats in the party. It must, instead, look inwards and address the fault lines at various levels. The idealist in Rahul Gandhi should know that nothing empowers a party more than the leader's largeness of heart.

At the same time and in the best traditions of democratic politics, the ruling parties in Haryana and Jammu and Kashmir are expected to respect the voice of the Opposition and remember the abiding lesson of history that time is intolerant of hubris. Lest the proponents of the virtues of 'realpolitik' forget, democratic politics is not morally neutral, and the nation's collective conscience asserts itself eventually.

7

Bulldozer Justice: Iron in the Nation's Soul[1]

The defence of democracy and the rule of law is the collective burden of the people as a whole.

1. *Frontline Magazine* (25 September 2024); Published as 'Don't let the State trample over the law of the land' in The *Tribune* (23 September 2024).

The Supreme Court's interim order of 17 September 2024, staying the demolition of properties of persons accused in criminal cases, is premised on the unexceptionable principle of constitutional governance that the exercise of state power is accountable to the discipline of the Constitution. It is a reminder to executive authorities that in a state government by the rule of law, mere lip service to procedural niceties is not sufficient assurance of substantive compliance with the mandatory requirements of legal due process. The Court's order, rooted in "the ethos of the Constitution", echoes the outraged conscience of the nation against the State's exercise of brute force in meting out retributive justice. That the order was resisted in Court by the government in a matter seen as a frontal assault on constitutional conscience and an indelible scar on the soul of the nation speaks for itself.

The Court's intervention in a petition filed by the Jamiat Ulama-i-Hind in the wake of widely reported demolitions across the country was sought on the touchstone of Article 21 of the Constitution that guarantees to all individuals the right to life with dignity, which includes the right to shelter, privacy and reputation. Though belated, the Court's order interdicts what is now infamously known as "bulldozer justice", a punitive mode wholly incompatible with the first principles of constitutional justice. In a purposive judicial intervention, the Court proposed a set of guidelines on a "Pan India Basis" to prevent unlawful demolitions anywhere in the country and has exercised its plenary jurisdiction to fill a legal vacuum. In a perfect harmonising of equities, it has been ruled that the injunction regarding demolitions would not apply in cases of encroachment of public spaces such as "road, footpath, abutting railway line or any river body or water bodies and also to cases where there is an order for demolition made by the court…"

It is worrisome that the apex Court's intervention came after several residential and commercial premises were unlawfully razed, in what is prima facie a legally indefensible action across several states such as Uttar Pradesh, Madhya Pradesh, Haryana, Maharashtra and Delhi. Even as attempts to justify "bulldozer justice" persist, the unlawful use of brutal force by executive authorities to deprive citizens of their homes and places of work has shamed the nation. We are compelled to ask ourselves if there is "fair play for poor as well as for rich, for private individuals as well as government officials" and whether "the right of the individual, subject to his duties to the State, be maintained, asserted and exalted" (from Winston Churchil's 1938 pre-war speech, expounding the necessary conditions of democracy).

Clearly, as long as the sanctity of our homes is not secure against unjust state intrusion, the cherished ideal of Gandhi's Swaraj and a vision of libertarian democracy in which "…the poorest man may in his cottage bid defiance to all the force of the crown…" will remain a distant dream. Discriminatory, disproportionate, arbitrary and violative of the rule of law, "bulldozer justice" is an anathema in any civilised society, especially in a country whose political and social consciousness has been shaped in the crucible of a long and arduous struggle for freedom against the oppressive colonial rule.

In the cause that is yet to be argued, the Court is expected to respond to the constitutional command in an unapologetic assertion of its remit. Summoned to defend fundamental freedoms, it must revalidate its role as the nation's impartial judicial arbiter by scripting a credible remedy that will minimise, if not eliminate, the excesses of the state against its citizens.

But the issue at hand raises larger questions: Must citizens be compelled to approach the highest Court for relief against the recurring high-handedness of the executive branch? Can a constitutional state sanction retribution through processes unknown to law and extend the consequences to innocent family members of the accused, including women, children and the elderly, depriving them of a roof over their head and the means of subsistence? Implicit in the interrogatory is a perceived perversion of constitutional governance at different levels, which compels an urgent review of the nation's governing processes to ensure that administrative justice meets the test of fairness.

While the courts can be expected to perform their assigned task, it would be unfair to impose a disproportionate burden on the judiciary, considering the institutional limitations. The defence of democracy and the rule of law is, after all, the collective burden of the three wings of the Indian state and, in the ultimate analysis, of the people as a whole, who must write their own story through peaceful democratic assertion against unjust actions of the state. As a repository of the people's power, the government is expected to exercise its authority in demonstrable compliance with established legal procedures so that justice is not only done but is also seen to be done.

We must confront a broader question: Is the smallness of our politics conducive to the establishment of a just society? Indeed, it is necessary to state the obvious and ask difficult questions, lest we forget who we are. No apologies are owed for condemning the unacceptable, particularly the inhuman acts that have wounded national sensitivities and have left behind an unhealable pain in an unending "daze of grief". By a robust refusal to countenance injustice and abuse of power, Justices B.R. Gavai and K.V. Vishwanathan have once again vindicated the oath of their high office. In their path-breaking judgments on bail and "bulldozer justice", the judges have validated the view of the distinguished historian Arnold Toynbee that the history of human civilisation is the history of how civilisations respond to challenges that shape the world. The tragedy of "bulldozer justice"[2] and the Court's action will doubtless define the future course of India's democracy.

---

2. Despite the highest Court's ruling, razing of homes and buildings by bulldozers deployed by the executive authorities without compliance with the legal due process, have been reported in some states.

8

Lest We Forget[1]

Justice as the ultimate virtue is '...a standard to achieve and an ideal to reach.'

1. Published as 'The Court sends a message' in *Indian Express* (4 September 2024), *Hindustan Times* (Hindi) (4 September 2024).

Given the nation's current preoccupation with a sense of fear and disquiet over the oppressive processes of our criminal justice system, the Supreme Court's recent pronouncements regarding the grant of bail in cases brought under stringent penal statutes have come as a welcome relief. The decisions have given hope to the accused against unconscionable deprivation of their liberty, reputation and privacy. The judgments speak for themselves.

In Manish Kumar Sisodia v. The Directorate of Enforcement (9 August 2024), the Court expounded upon its mandate "…to lean in favour of constitutionalism and the rule of law of which liberty is an intrinsic path…" It further held that "bail is the rule and jail an exception", with the right to fair and speedy trial as implicit in the right to life under Article 21 of the Constitution. Following its eloquent exposition of the constitutional position in Sisodia, the Court, speaking through Justice B.R. Gavai in Kavitha v. The Directorate of Enforcement (27 August 2024) reiterated that the "fundamental right to liberty provided under Article

21 … is superior to statutory restrictions…" and that "…prolonged incarceration before being pronounced guilty of an offence should not be permitted to become punishment without trial…" Again, in Prem Prakash v. Union of India (28 August 2024), the Court speaking through Justice K.V. Vishwanathan, held that "liberty of the individual is always a rule and deprivation is the exception…" The Court ruled that "keeping a person behind bars for unlimited periods of time in the hope of speedy completion of trial would deprive the fundamental right of persons under Article 21…" A Bench of Justice Hrishikesh Roy and Justice S.V.N. Bhatti decided likewise in Vijay Nair v. The Directorate of Enforcement (2 September 2024), following the ratio of the earlier decisions and granted bail to the accused on account of a long confinement in custody and the accused's right to a speedy trial.

Significantly, while interpreting Section 45 of the Prevention of Money Laundering Act, 2002 (PMLA), the Court declared in Prem Prakash that the words "reasonable grounds for believing" therein require the court to see "if there is a genuine case against the accused…" based on "reasonable material collected during investigation…" In relation to the statement of the accused in custody under the PMLA, the Court reiterated that the person in custody "is not a person who can be considered as one operating with a free mind…" and that "it will be extremely unsafe to render such statements admissible against the maker, as such a course of action would be contrary to all cannons of fair play and justice…" In this context, the Court's judgment ought to persuade the government to revisit the law and judicial processes for mandatorily setting a reasonable maximum period of detention for the accused without trial.

By reading the stringent statutory provisions in the light of its fundamental rights jurisprudence, the Court affirmed the primacy of the Constitution and of Article 21 in the hierarchy of fundamental rights. In another case, Frank Vitus v. Narcotics Control Bureau and Ors. decided on 8 July 2023, under the Narcotic Drugs and Psychotropic Substances Act, 1985 (NDPS Act), the Court, speaking through Justice Abhay S. Oka, held that so long as the accused "is not held guilty, the presumption of innocence is applicable…" and that bail conditions that infringe the accused person's right to privacy will be violative of Article 21. It ruled further that a bail condition which is impossible for the accused to comply with cannot be imposed. Thus, by reading the necessary safeguards into the law, the apex Court, as the final constitutional arbiter, has decisively intervened to prevent infraction of the accused's fundamental rights during the course of criminal prosecutions. The distinguished judges demonstrating "patience and gravity of hearing" have shown judicial statesmanship by suggesting that laws, noble in intent, but perverted in their application and non-deferential to the constitutional command, cannot be the nation's way forward for combating corruption and crime.

The value of these important rulings is located not only in their unquestionable constitutional merit but also in the intellectual integrity of the distinguished judges who have aligned law with justice, thereby investing the voice of libertarians with an impregnable constitutional imprimatur. Founded in reason and the sacrosanctity of fundamental rights, these decisions will reinforce popular respect for law in its larger function as a stabilising force. In the interstices of these judgments is a reassuring message that voices against injustice, even though muffled, will be heard at last and that justice will not be suborned to the rigours of law unconscionably applied. The pronouncements by the highest constitutional Court are a resounding judicial affirmation that the latent tension between unaccountable power and liberty will be resolved in favour of the latter. These judgments affirm that justice as the ultimate virtue is "…a standard to achieve and an ideal to reach…"

The Court has vindicated justice, whose majesty is enshrined in one of the most cherished maxims of common law, "*Fiat justitia ruat caelum*" (Let justice be done, though heavens fall), and has validated its own standing as "supreme in the majesty of duty and power". Its jurisprudence on bail echoes the thought propounded by philosophers, including Edmund Burke, that freedom is a "…clause in the great primaeval contract of eternal society … which holds all physical and all moral natures each in their appointed place…" [Edmund Burke, *Reflections on the Revolution in France*, 1866].

However, the cause of constitutionalism can be best subserved only if constitutional courts can proactively ensure the enforcement of their seminal edicts to vitalise a living Constitution to fulfil its promise of a life of freedom and dignity for all. In an age defined by an absence of institutional deference, the authority of the court as the nation's moral arbiter will depend upon its readiness to hold the mirror to those in default of the Constitution and to reassure the nation that none will be condemned by accusation alone. Hopefully, the Court's proclaimed libertarian philosophy will nudge political parties to revisit their politics in deference to constitutional imperatives. Lest we forget, the defence of inalienable human rights is the collective burden of the people as a whole and the institutions established by them.

9

Let's Reawaken as a Nation to Sing the Song of Freedom[1]

Let us answer the summons of the Tiranga and honour its command without appropriating it for partisan ends.

1. The *Tribune*, 17 August 2024; *Punjabi Tribune* (Hindi), 24 August 2024.

Seventy-seven years after its "tryst with destiny", India has much to celebrate today. As the fastest-growing economy and the world's largest pluralist democracy that has succeeded in lifting millions of its citizens above abject poverty over the years, its voice is heard with respect in the chanceries of the world. Its imminent rise as the world's third-largest economy, its demonstrated scientific prowess, democratic resilience, and an exceptional cultural heritage of harmonious coexistence are reasons enough for every Indian to rejoice.

And yet, as we salute the Tiranga in reverence, on Independence Day and thereafter, we cannot forget that the road to national glory must navigate the harsh truth of unfreedom, violence and injustices that have scarred the soul of the nation. The heart-rending sight of a husband dragging his wife tied to his motorcycle with none showing the courage to stop the horrendous ordeal of a helpless woman, the rape and murder of a young lady doctor inside a Kolkata hospital, the unspeakable pain of the nation and of its wrestler daughter who lost an Olympic medal for the country over 100 grams of body weight despite her unremitting toil and discipline in the service of her chosen sport, and the forced migration of our youth to foreign lands for want of gainful employment, leaving behind old and often untended parents in the twilight of their lives tell a painful story. Recurring and aggravated discrimination on account of widening disparities in incomes, shameful display of wealth mocking the poverty of the wretched, continuing suicides by the impoverished, custodial torture of the helpless and the murderous police encounters in and outside police custody interrogate our claims as a welfare and liberal state.

The economic and social plight of the elderly on account of neglect by children, too caught up in pursuit of unguided ambition and material gain, loss of dignity of the marginalised even in death, the wrecking of reputations, privacy and dignity of individuals in media without a meaningful recourse and social consciousness generally immune to the misery of the destitute, is not the Bharat of Bapu's dreams who, along with his compatriots had envisioned an egalitarian society in which we could live in the shelter of each other, joined together in empathy. Heightened religious strife, escalating caste and regional conflicts, bitter political animosities beyond ideological contestation, and the abuse of state power to settle personal scores question the health of Indian democracy.

Having celebrated the anniversary of Independence—the day when we unshackled ourselves from the yoke of British colonialism and were reborn into freedom—we must ask ourselves whether we have vindicated the aspirations of a free people for justice and dignity. We must also reflect on whether the present state of our democracy is such as can translate into reality the vision of our founders and ourselves, and whether the conduct of an elevating democratic politics is at all possible without its anchor in public morality, as the Father of the Nation never tired of reminding us. The need to repurpose the nation's politics is compelling, and lest we forget the lesson of history, there can be no democracy without humanity; both are integral to each other. While we celebrate our freedom, let us think of the marginalised masses, whose sufferings question our gains beyond apology. Let us shed a tear for their unbearable pain born out of undeserved deprivation, denial and unending injustices.

In drawing attention to the bitter truth of our reality, 77 years after freedom, the idea is not to apportion blame but to correct the nation's course for the future, as also to remind ourselves that the purpose of human life and freedom is to battle for succour to those bearing the brunt of misery in a life without hope. While I yearn to sing the song of freedom aloud, I find my voice muffled by the deafening cries of pain and grief that "wells up like a lump in the throat". The reality of hunger, poverty, exploitation and misery of the multitude does not leave me free to exult at this moment. My thoughts take me to the tireless exertions of our founding fathers who sacrificed themselves so that we may live with honour today and hereafter. They now lie in the dark, their dreams unrealised and memories maligned.

Let us endeavour collectively to ensure that our politics is inspired by magnanimity, without being held hostage to the "vice of shallowness" and is inspired by high purpose. Let us answer the summons of the Tiranga and honour its command without appropriating it for partisan ends. Indeed, this must be the moment of national reawakening, to shed the intellectual amorality of our politics and to invest the powerless with power to script their destiny. Only then can we sing together the song of freedom. Only then will the power of joy overcome the stillness of despair.

10

A Custodian of Liberty[1]

The nation must repurpose its politics away from personal animosities in an elevating pursuit of justice and dignity for all.

1. The *Hindu* 13 August 2024

Former deputy chief minister of Delhi Manish Sisodia's enlargement on bail by the Supreme Court of India, after an unconscionably long incarceration, is a welcome vindication of the apex Court's remit as custodian of individual liberties. In an eloquent exposition of its mandate, the Court reiterated that "a Constitutional court has to lean in favour of constitutionalism and the rule of law of which liberty is an intrinsic part..." Citing its judgment in Arnab Manoranjan Goswami v. State of Maharashtra & Ors (2020),[2] it reaffirmed that "liberty across human eras is as tenacious as tenacious can be". Reiterating the salutary constitutional principle expounded as early as 1977 by Justice V.R. Krishna Iyer, that bail is the rule and jail an exception, the Court reaffirmed that the right to fair and speedy trial was implicit in the right to life under Article 21. It concluded that this right was denied to the erstwhile deputy chief minister of Delhi. In arriving at its conclusions, the Court relied on the observations of the Court in its first order of 30 October 2023 (Manish

2. AIR 2021 SUPREME COURT 1

Sisodia v. Central Bureau of Investigation), and also the submissions advanced before it in the first round, adverting particularly to the 56,000 pages of documents and 456 witnesses (at that stage which numbers were subsequently increased) in the two cases—and which the Court felt could delay the trial and conclusion of the case inordinately. It also referred to and relied upon several of its judgments from Kashmira Singh (1977)[3] till the later decisions, in P. Chidambaram (2020)[4] and Satendar Kumar Antil (2022)[5] on the accused's right to speedy trial. To these could be added the Court's decision in Sheikh Javed Iqbal (2024).[6] Stating further that the constitutional mandate must prevail as the higher law, the apex Court ruled, in Manish Sisodia v. The Directorate of Enforcement,[7] purposively that "the right to bail in cases of delay, coupled with incarceration for a long period, depending on the nature of the allegations, should be read into Section 439 CrPC and Section 45 of the PMLA".

In its entirety, the judgment must gladden the hearts of libertarians, considering the troubling and persistent apprehensions about the weaponisation of

---

3. 1977 AIR 2147
4. AIR 2019 SC 5272
5. 10 SCC 51 (2022)
6. 2024 INSC 534
7. 2024 INSC 595

the stringent penal laws in the country, including the PMLA. Taking cognizance of the information furnished to the Parliament recently, the Supreme Court noticed that out of the over 5000 cases brought under the PMLA in the last 10 years, only forty cases resulted in convictions. In his statement in the Rajya Sabha, the Minister of State for Finance disclosed that "the ED filed 15 Enforcement Case Information Reports (ECIRs) in 2019, followed by 28 in 2020, 26 in 2021, 34 in 2022, 26 in 2023 and 3 in 2024 as on 31July. Only one conviction in the cases was reported to have been made in 2020." Clearly, the processes of our criminal justice system leading to endless delays are oppressive, with procedure itself being the punishment. The reality of the technicalities of procedural laws defeating justice has been judicially recognised and eloquently summed up as "the mortality of justice at the hands of law" in Sushil Kumar Sen (1975)[8] and Rani Kusum (2005).[9]

A Caveat

Notwithstanding its unexceptionable constitutional merit, the judgment raises a troubling question. Was it right for the Court, consistent with its other observations in the first round, to condone the custodial

8. 1975 AIR 1185

9. (2005)6 SCC 705

confinement of the accused based on the statement of the prosecution that the trial would be completed within six to eight months? Or to extend the detention of the accused on the basis of the prosecuting counsel's statement recorded in the Court's second order of 4 June 2024, that the complaint/charge-sheet would be filed on or before 3 July 2024? In a sense, does this not make the prosecutor a judge in its own cause, contrary to the first principles of natural justice and vitiating at its core the procedural imperatives of fair trial?

In our constitutional scheme, the liberty of individuals cannot be held hostage to the benevolence or sense of fairness of the prosecutor alone. It must stand on the unbreachable foundation of justice anchored in inalienable rights "born in flesh, carried in our bodies from birth to death". We know that sacrosanct rights "undergird" the law; that there is no virtue in legal processes that are unjust, and laws that fail to render justice must be changed. Denial of freedom is denial of humanity itself. Therefore, its preservation against excesses of the executive is the first charge on the apex Court's constitutional and moral authority. Although the ultimate guarantee of civil liberties lies in the faith and assertion of the people, as Justice Robert Jackson of the United States reminded us in Douglas v. City of Jeannette (1943), the courts' auxiliary protection against encroachment of human rights is the crucial test of a vibrant democracy.

In eventually restoring Mr Sisodia's liberty pending the final decision in his case, the apex Court has redeemed itself of the charge of ambivalence in the earlier rounds despite the existence of a legal and factual basis for bail. It need not now "trudge on the debris of conscience". The judgment would have served its purpose if undertrials were not made to languish in custody endlessly with their freedom, reputation, privacy, and dignity irretrievably lost without apology or recompense. And, the nation must repurpose its politics away from personal animosities in an ennobling pursuit of justice and dignity for all, thereby revitalising a democracy under stress.

11

Artificial Intelligence: The Ethical and Constitutional Boundaries[1]

Human dignity must remain at the pinnacle, as the ultimate civilisational aspiration.

1. Published as 'Set Ethical, Constitutional Boundaries' in The *Tribune* 13 July 2024, *Punjabi Tribune* (Punjabi), 17 July 2024, 'The Moral Algorithm' in *Open Magazine*, 29 July 2024.

Artificial Intelligence (AI), as the transformative technological revolution of our age, attests to mankind's unrelenting pursuit of understanding, controlling and remaking the world in the image of its changing aspirations, an endeavour not without its challenges.

The apprehended evisceration of core human values and dehumanising of the society itself has invited a raging global debate about the ethical challenges posed by AI and the possibility of an effective international regulatory regime to discipline its deployment. Several regional and global initiatives have, therefore, focused on limiting the use of AI within the larger moral framework of human rights to harmoniously moderate technological exuberance with compelling moral restraints.

The Montreal Declaration on the ethics of intelligence systems; proceedings of the ACM FAccT Conferences; UNESCO's Global Standards on AI Ethics (Recommendation on the Ethics of Artificial Intelligence), adopted by all the 193 member states in November 2021; the Biden Administration's non-binding AI Bill of Rights (AIBOR); European Union legislation on AI; congressional hearings in the United States and deliberations of the national regulatory bodies confirm the seriousness of ethical challenges within the AI ecosystem. Initiatives, such as the Global Observatory on the effect of AI, Global Forum on Ethics of AI, AI Ethics Experts without Borders (AIEB) and Women for AI Ethics (W4 AI Ethics) have contributed towards a sharper understanding of the ethical issues involved.

History proclaims that at every step on the stairway to progress, humankind has made choices to define the progress of civilisation as the deepening of humanity and happiness of the people. The benefits of AI's positive contribution for the betterment of global health and educational systems, combating challenges of climate change, terrorism, cybercrime, pandemics, and natural disasters, etc., are transformative in the progressive evolution of human civilisation. Even so, there is an overwhelming consensus amongst stakeholders to tame the excesses of AI. It is rightly argued that the celebration of our technological triumphs cannot be a "mourning amidst the ruins" of humanity. Since all knowledge must be measured in terms of the values it advances, the use of AI demands evaluation in the framework of the prevailing ethical standards.

AI's known encroachment of our inalienable rights to freedom, privacy of emotions and intimate relationships, individual autonomy, the sacrosanctity of mental processes and individual consciousness, recognised as fundamental human rights in democracies across the world, is viewed as "part of the crisis of humanity". Grave concerns about AI-enabled manipulation of behavioral and electoral processes, the hacking of language to disrupt genuine democratic discourse, the challenge of deepfakes, intended and unintended biases for and against a class of the people by exploiting their vulnerabilities, including age, gender, disabilities and ethnicity, and the compounding of prevailing inequalities (such as the digital divide) are real. Serious apprehensions have been expressed about AI's ability "to effectively reshape history". Concerns about "overgrazing of the internet commons by rapacious technology companies" to maximise profit at the cost of data privacy and transparency abound.

That the AI leviathan needs to be regulated across geographical boundaries by an internationally enforceable legal code is evident in the recent comments of the principal AI entrepreneurs. Elon Musk is reported to have warned that "when we build AI without a kill switch, we are summoning the devil". Mark Zuckerberg has cautioned that "...the world will become more digital than physical. And that is not necessarily the best thing for human society". Apple co-founder Steve Wozniak has, in an open letter, suggested the acceleration of the development of a "robust AI governance system". Evidently, such a mechanism cannot be limited to self-regulation and should have effective mechanisms to fix accountability for transgression of the mandated red lines. It is, indeed, necessary to navigate the shadows of science if we are to bask in the glory of its illumination.

Whether or not these concerns are exaggerated, the predominant opinion on the subject is that in crafting our perspectives on the future of AI, we must accept that the elevating advance of human civilisation is located in humankind's unswerving commitment to the moral autonomy and rationality of the individual that recognises the primacy of the ideals of human dignity, inclusion, equality, freedom and justice. In the ongoing global debate on the ethical and moral framework within which AI must operate, doubts have been expressed on whether AI machines can serve as moral agents in "translating human moral complexity into an algorithmic form" or are capable of making ethical judgements as "full ethical agents" with the human understanding of ethics. It is imperative to erect unbreachable boundaries around AI to ensure that man remains the master of his universe and that sacred private spaces of the head and the heart remain sacrosanct in an age "which levels everything and reveres nothing".

Hopefully, the Global IndiaAI Summit held on 3 and 4 July 2024 in New Delhi will generate ideas for the responsible development and deployment of ethical and inclusive AI. It is for us to reaffirm that civilisation at its peak is about the elevation of man in the fullness of human glory, not in a tragic denouement of humanist morality. Our ability to secure a convergence in the prescription of scientists and philosophers for a humane world order will be an enduring contribution to this mission. And how we deal with this epochal challenge will define the quality of leadership and the hierarchy of moral values in which human dignity must remain at the pinnacle, as the ultimate civilisational aspiration.[2]

---

2. At a G-7 Summit in Canada (June 2025) Prime Minister Modi reiterated that "...we must adopt a human-centric approach. Everyone recognises the potential of AI. However, the real challenge is ensuring that AI tools enhance human dignity and empowerment ... we must work towards governance at an international level that addresses concerns related to AI while promoting innovation..." (*Indian Express*, New Delhi, 19 June 2025)

sacrosanct in an age which levels everything and reveres nothing.

Hopefully the Global IndiaAI Summit held on 3 and 4 July 2024 in New Delhi will generate ideas for the responsible development and deployment of ethical and inclusive AI. It is for us to reaffirm that civilisation at its peak is about the elevation of man in the fullness of human glory, not in a tragic denouement of humanist morality. Our ability to secure a convergence in the prescription of scientists and philosophers for a humane world order will be an enduring contribution to this mission. And how we deal with this epochal challenge will define the quality of leadership and the hierarchy of moral values in which human dignity must remain at the pinnacle, as the ultimate civilisational aspiration.[9]

7 At the G7 Summit in Canada (June 2025) Prime Minister Modi reiterated that "we must adopt a human-centric approach. Everyone recognises the [illegible] potential of AI. However, the real challenge is ensuring that AI [illegible] human dignity and empowerment [illegible] we must work towards governance [illegible]

9 [illegible] international level that addresses concerns related to AI while promoting innovation [illegible] New Delhi, 19 June 2025.

12

What the PM Must Do[1]

Power is a trust held on the condition that its exercise is just.

1. *Indian Express* (7 June 2024), *Ajit* (6 June 2024), *Dainik Tribune* (11 June 2024), *Punjabi Tribune* (11 June 2024)

In what is a clear moral victory for the Congress-led opposition, the 2024 mandate was a vote for democracy, dignity and justice. The result reflected the nation's distrust of concentrated power and an irrevocable commitment to constitutional fundamentals, emphasised in the manifesto of the Congress. The verdict was a tribute to the latent wisdom of the people sworn to freedom and liberty. It seems that the suppressed soul of the nation had found utterance, and the pledge we took on the midnight of freedom for the defence of liberty and dignity of the people is a continuing one. The electoral verdict affirmed an abiding lesson of democratic politics that the anguish of those affronted and alienated cannot be suppressed by a muscular state.

As the fulcrum of the opposition alliance, Congress led a vigorous pushback, making significant gains in the process. The results also confirmed the assertion of regional aspirations, considering the winning performance of most regional parties. The election signalled a reconfiguration of national politics and validated the Gandhis' leadership of the grand old party.

Most importantly, the results affirmed the integrity of the electoral process of the world's largest democracy. The vindication of democracy was the seminal message of this election.

However, congratulations are due to the prime minister for the NDA's eventual victory at the hustings. He virtually carried the election on his shoulders, demonstrating a remarkable tenacity of purpose throughout the gruelling campaign. His crowning as a democratically elected leader of the world's largest democracy for the third consecutive term was indeed an exceptional event in the history of India's contemporary politics. Despite the setback, the prime minister can claim consolation in the fact that the BJP has established itself as a pan-Indian political party with a pole position in national politics, significantly increasing its vote share in the southern states.

However, the election presented a formidable challenge for the prime minister. The nation, fatigued and divided by a fractious election and a scarred soul, needs to be healed. The alienation of minorities, a demeaning electoral discourse, the perversion of legal and judicial processes in pursuit of political ends, the abuse of constitutional power by ruling parties across the country and rampant corruption at all levels are unmistakable signs of a flailing democracy and a debilitated polity. The foremost task for the prime minister, therefore, is to refurbish the nation's credentials as a constitutional democracy anchored in a demonstrated commitment to the rule of law and justice. As holder of the highest executive office, the prime minister must speak for the nation as a whole. He must use his personal chemistry with the vast section of Indian people to burnish his vision for the nation with a proclaimed commitment to fraternity and the dignity of all citizens. He is expected to be magnanimous and accommodative of the dissenting views of his political opponents in the best traditions of democracy. And he must effectuate the principle of equal citizenship in a pluralist society.

The prime minister, at the head of a coalition government, will need to seek and secure the widest possible consensus on matters impacting overarching national interests. The nature of the mandate signalled a cooperative enterprise for national renewal premised on the politics of reconciliation. The primary responsibility for this rests with the prime minister as a leader of the nation. In this endeavour, he will necessarily need the constructive cooperation of the Opposition, which represents a large section of the nation. The Opposition, on its part, cannot be cynical and compulsively critical of every action of the government. It must respect the mandate to preserve its credibility in public estimation. And it cannot also be seen as graceless at this hour.

Indeed, the protagonists of Dr B.R. Ambedkar must not forget his message that in a constitutional democracy, there is no scope for anarchist politics.

The mandate of 2024, which deepened Indian democracy, should yield policies that enjoy widespread acceptance and governance that brings the nation together in addressing the daunting challenges of our age, including a pervasive assault on fundamental freedoms through the arbitrary exercise of power. In his promised plan of action by the new government in the coming days, the prime minister may wish to consider repealing or amending the oppressive penal laws that are routinely abused in derogation of citizens' constitutional rights and enacting humanitarian laws, including the much-awaited comprehensive anti-custodial legislation.

Above all, the prime minister, at the head of the new government, will doubtless reflect on the lesson of history, that power is a trust held on the condition that its exercise is just, and such as would enhance the moral autonomy of free citizens to grasp their freedom.

13

Keeping the Constitutional Faith[1]

The inviolability of freedom depends on the moral courage, fearlessness and magnanimity of its defenders.

1. Published as 'This election is a litmus test of our collective wisdom' in The *Tribune* 17 May 2024, *Dainik Jagran* (Hindi) 16 May 2024.

With the conclusion of the fourth phase of Lok Sabha elections on 13 May 2024, the electoral fate of contestants from 379 of the 543 seats seeking election to the highest forum of Indian democracy is sealed in the ballot boxes. The election, seen as transformative of the nation's political landscape, is witnessing a spirited pushback to the Modi regime from the INDIA bloc, even as the ruling dispensation led by the Prime Minister has had a clear head start in scripting its campaign theme.

The Opposition's counter-narrative, focused on the defence of constitutional democracy and its concomitant values, is premised on the authoritarian impulses of a muscular state that negate the first principles of liberal democracy and accountability of power encased in the nation's republican charter. The unprecedented arrests across India of the ruling regime's key political adversaries, a demonstrable decline of constitutional institutions, a captive bureaucracy and a generally obsequious media are cited in support. Ensuring a national resonance for its inspirational narrative is the principal challenge for the Opposition.

Regrettably, the diminishing and debilitating tone of a cacophonic campaign on both sides seems to have drowned the real issues, with abuse and calumny substituting for reason and contestation. The perversion of democratic discourse helmed by leaders unable to rise above themselves attests to a flailing democracy. The pursuit of power for its appellations alone, with scant regard for its ends and a cynical deriding of political idealism as a utopian dream to be argued out of consciousness, presents the electoral exercise as clothing the pursuit of personal ambitions with a semblance of democratic legitimacy.

If indeed the BJP and the Opposition consider this election as a watershed moment that will determine the future of the country, they must continue to focus public attention on core national issues.

The INDIA bloc, speaking in multiple voices, cannot forget "the plain lesson of history, that the wants of men will only secure recognition to the point that they are forcibly articulate…" as Harold Laski put it. The power of a clear statement is critical for the success of the Opposition's campaign. Apart from an unrelenting focus on its core campaign theme, communicated and made intelligible to each voter, the alliance cannot shirk the critical question of an alternate leadership of the nation. Congress, as the principal Opposition party, has advisedly chosen not to formally present its chief campaigner, Rahul Gandhi, as the prime ministerial candidate. Whatever the limitations and logic of the situation, the question of leadership will be critical to the outcome of the campaign, flawed comparisons with the past notwithstanding. As a necessary condition of revitalising itself to serve as the fulcrum of Opposition unity, the grand old party must recognise the distinction between servility and loyalty of its members. Only then can it reclaim the willing allegiance of its alienated cadres. In its internal functioning, it must listen magnanimously to "the hidden silences". Evidently, a self-effacing humility and generosity of heart to heal the erasures of conscience are critical attributes of leadership needed for national renewal.

The prime minister, as the chief campaigner and torchbearer of his party's ideology, has demonstrated an exceptional tenacity of purpose and will to prevail against the combined Opposition of 26 parties. He has strategically anchored his party's campaign in a sentiment of national glory, hope for the people in their future and their emotional sensitivities, and may well win a third consecutive term in office. But he would, in his wisdom, know that the idea of justice, dignity and freedom outlive the seduction of power. As the leader of a nation defined by its diversity, he must accept that his primary obligation is to nurture a unifying politics to sustain national unity and bridge the myriad socio-political divides. Electoral victory must mean more than an arithmetical majority. Irrespective of who forms the government, the victory goal must belong to those whose politics and votes sustain and strengthen a democracy founded on justice and human dignity. We are entitled to aspire for a democracy in which all of us can hold our heads high as empowered citizens of an enlightened nation that seeks to be the Vishwaguru.

In this aspirational view of our common future, there is no scope for narrowness of mind, wilfulness or transient responses to political exigencies at the cost of the nation's foundational principles. In this moment of test, those who stand on the side of freedom will find themselves on the right side of history. This election, seen as a historic milestone in the life of the nation, will test our collective wisdom on how we establish justice as the primary goal of social and political institutions and the basis of a democratic state.

The election is about reinforcing the values of equal citizenship and ensuring that the power sought in the name of the people is used in furtherance of their inherent rights. It will define the land and its people, who alone must mediate their future, remembering that the inviolability of freedom depends on the moral courage, fearlessness and magnanimity of its defenders. This election cannot be about one's own victimhood. It must, instead, heal the deepening fissures in our social fabric so that we can claim that Indian democracy is not a beguiling dream.

14

Justice Delayed, Empathy Denied[1]

Justice is the first virtue of social institutions.
– John Rawls

1. *Indian Express*,12 March 2024; *Jag Bani*, 17 March 2024; *Punjab Kesari*, 17 March 2024; *Navodya Times*, 17 March 2024; *Hind Samachar*, 17 March 2024.

On 7 March 2025, Professor G.N. Saibaba walked to freedom after a 10-year-long incarceration, declared by the Nagpur bench of the Bombay High Court as illegal on 5 March. Rejecting the charge against all the accused of aiding members of a banned organisation to wage war against the Government of India, the Court held that their detention, including that of the wheelchair-bound handicapped academic, was unsustainable in law. The judgment, based on a piercing scrutiny of the law and evidence on record, is a welcome, albeit belated, affirmation of the Constitution's libertarian promise. We are reminded that a reflective intellectual engagement with political doctrines cannot, in itself, be a basis of criminality, consistent with the fundamental human right to free speech and thought.

That freedom came to Saibaba and others after suffering long years of a "brutal" life in unlawful custody is a painful reminder of a grave institutional deficit. The illegal custody of the accused, facilitated by an insensitive persistence by enforcers of the state to keep them—including a physically challenged academic—in prison, questions the fairness of the nation's administrative and judicial processes. Particularly worrisome and wholly unconscionable is the Supreme Court's earlier order in 2022 restoring Saibaba to custody after setting aside his discharge by the High Court and hearing the state's appeal on a holiday.

The turns and twists in the case have tested the boundaries of state power and the resilience of our judicial processes to vindicate the constitutional conscience. In a resounding and reasoned rejection of the state's case, the Court held that merely downloading information about "Naxal philosophy" or even sympathising with their philosophy would not invite the rigours of the UAPA and that the prosecution had failed to establish an active role of the accused with particular incidents of violence and terrorism. The Court scoffed at "vague allegations" pressed by the prosecution as the basis of a criminal conviction and thereby reaffirmed the first principles of criminal jurisprudence.

However, the treatment meted out to the severely disabled professor, unable even to attend to his most private needs without assistance, and his detention for 10 long years in preventive custody without conviction under anti-terrorism legislation, begs several disturbing questions. Clearly, the oppressiveness of the judicial process, which in itself is the punishment, is a profoundly important and unaddressed issue impacting the quality of justice in criminal trials. The absence of even a hint of compassion in the dispensation of justice to a person physically, financially and emotionally vulnerable to the vagaries of a criminal trial questions the foundational idea of judicial justice rooted in empathy and reason. The prosecution's case that a person with Saibaba's disabilities could be a threat to the security of the country and government, based on his ideological preferences, incredulous as it is, became the basis of a citizen's loss of liberty to an unacceptably long confinement behind prison walls. Whether this result is consistent with the republic's sense of constitutional justice is a pertinent interrogatory. Must we suffer legal processes that yield injustice and for which there is no recompense? This remains a larger question in search of a meaningful political and social response.

The long and arduous incarceration of a handicapped accused, facilitated by an oppressive criminal justice system, has understandably attracted wide public attention. The loss of reputation and dignity of the accused and a soul-scarring sense of humiliating helplessness in the face of pervasive injustice must awaken the public to collectively assert their right to, as John Rawls put it, "justice, as the first virtue of social institutions".

The message of the Saibaba case is that a nation committed to the freedom of its citizens and the pursuit of human dignity cannot remain indifferent to a system in which justice is defeated and dignity compromised. Indifference to the absence of even-handed justice questions the nation's aspiration for a just democracy driven by credible laws and served by institutional constraints against the arbitrary exercise of state power. Will the Saibaba case and its lessons be relegated to the margins of our memories and allowed to fade away in time, or will it serve as a transformative moment in an unending "pilgrimage to justice"? This is the defining question of our times. Since the history of nations is shaped by events that unfold over time, this case should be a watershed moment towards a renaissance of our cultural heritage rooted in benign justice and empathy for the weak. We know that the fate of freedom depends upon a collective assertion of its moral force that lends it legitimacy as a constitutional right. And lest we forget, the enduring lesson of history is that the idea of freedom survives the ravages of tyranny.

The refusal of the apex Court to stay the order of acquittal in this case holds out hope that the top Court will reclaim its custody of the Constitution. Bound by the fetters of their remit, constitutional institutions are indeed expected to vindicate justice and be seen to be doing so.

15

Judicial Clarity on Free Speech[1]

Falsehood flies, and truth comes limping after it.
–Jonathan Swift

1. *The Hindu*, 21 February 2024; *Punjabi Tribune*, 23 January 2024; *Hind* (Urdu), 26 February 2024; *Jag Bani* (Punjabi), 26 February 2024.

The 31 January 2024 decision of Justice Gautam Patel of the Bombay High Court in a bunch of petitions, popularly known as Kunal Kamra's case, stands out for its compelling articulation of the constitutional fundamentals in relation to the right of free speech on "social media". Uncoerced by the climate of our times, the learned judge has reiterated the sacrosanctity of the inviolate constitutional guarantee of free speech, not to be tinkered with or read down, except for the reasonable restrictions thereon as envisaged in Article 19(2), (6) of the Constitution. The affirmation of this constitutional right and its eloquent defence against state encroachment by the distinguished judge is reassuring, even though his decision on the subject is not yet binding, because of a split verdict by the Division Bench.

The context of the decision is the amended Rule 3(1)(b)(v) of the IT Rules 2021, widely perceived as arbitrary and unjust. Relevant extracts of the rule are reproduced below:

3(1) … (b) the intermediary … shall make reasonable efforts by itself, and to cause the users of its computer resource to not host, display, upload, modify, publish, transmit, store, update or share any information that…

(v) …in respect of any business of the Central Government, is identified as fake or false or misleading by such fact check unit of the Central Government as the Ministry may, by notification published in the Official Gazette, specify.

Failure to comply with the due diligence obligation under the above amended rule would invite penal consequences for the errant intermediary under Rule 7, reproduced below:

"Rule 7: Where an intermediary fails to observe these rules … the intermediary shall be liable for punishment under any law for the time being in force, including the provisions of the Act and the Indian Penal Code."

The combined effect of these provisions is to confer unfettered powers on the government-appointed Fact Check Unit (FCU) to control the digital content in matters connected with the business of the Central government, without specifying the contours of the government's business.

Drawing upon scholarly treatises, the Supreme Court's celebrated jurisprudence enunciated inter alia, in Shreya Singhal (2015), K.S. Puttaswamy (2019), Anuradha Bhasin (2020) et al, the history of the Constitution's libertarian lineage and philosophy of constitutional democracy. Justice Patel's decision vindicates the nation's hope that despite occasional missteps, our constitutional courts can be trusted with the custody of our fundamental rights and can navigate the challenges of the digital age in relation to the right of free speech, as the driving force of a liberal democracy.

Declaring the amended rule as unconstitutional, Justice Patel held that the amendment results in a form of censorship of user content, is vague and overbroad, destructive of the right to criticise and debate, does not disclose reasonable standards and objective criteria to determine the validity of the decisions of the FCU as the sole decision maker, that the amendment is not within the boundaries of reasonable restrictions envisaged in Article 19(2), (6) and that the impugned amendment was unconstitutional for infracting the rule of non-arbitrariness and non-discrimination in Article 14, absent, "clear guidance" and non-application of the rule to the print media. Invoking, amongst other principles, the doctrine of proportionality and the absolute necessity of the measure to achieve the state's goal, the judge held the amended rule as ultra vires

Article 19(1)(a), 19(2), 19(1)(g), 19(6), Article 14 and Section 79 of the IT Act.

The decision of the learned judge vindicates the constitutional conscience in as much as it scoffs at "the potential for wanton abuse" of untrammelled power, a view wholly consistent with the first principles of constitutional governance. The capping glory of the decision rests on the judge's elevating enunciation of the democratic principle that "the cacophony of dissent and disagreement is the symphony of a democracy at work…" The resounding rejection of the impugned amendment for its "chilling effect" (Shreya Singhal, 2015; Zeran, 1997) and "a frontal assault on the marketplace of ideas" is the judge's welcome message that fear-instilled stillness ill serves the case of a vibrant democracy.

Importantly, the decision does not discount the need for regulation of digital platforms. Indeed, there can be no doubt about the imperative of combatting fakery and misinformation, which are not only a threat to democracy but also to the indefeasible right to the reputation and dignity of individuals. The truth of Jonathan Swift's statement in 1710 that "Falsehood flies, and truth comes limping after it," was never more pronounced than now, in the age of the internet.

This decision of Justice Patel is, in its essence, a repudiation of the unreasonably wide ambit and discriminatory nature of the regulatory power under the amended rule and protection against the imminent potential of its abuse. It represents a just balance between "the abyss of unrestrained power" and the "heaven of freedom". The decision validates the logic of judicial review as a bulwark against the excesses of majoritarian assemblies and untamed power. It reaffirms the foundational premise of a democratic state that "the will of the State is subject to scrutiny by those who are affected by the exercise of State power and that democratic power" is "a trust held upon conditions" to secure the inherent rights of the people (Harold Laski, *A Grammar of Politics*, 1937). The judgment tells us that in times of executive-centred governance, a law that permits its enforcers to become agents of injustice cannot be countenanced in a constitutional democracy.

The clarity of thought, the power of a clear statement and its unexceptionable constitutional premise lend a unique quality to a defining judicial decision, which represents a convergence of constitutional principles and the nation's felt sensitivities about the critical right of free speech as a necessary condition of freedom. Hopefully, its irrefutable rationale will attain judicial finality before long. In the interregnum, it is hoped that the Central government will heed the reported suggestion of the Judge (7 February) to the Centre, not to notify and operationalise the amended/impugned rule. The tradition of deference to judicial decisions in complex matters of significant import and expectation of self-restraint on the part of the government to foster inter-institutional comity demands that the impugned amendment to Rule 3(1)(b)(v) of the IT Rules 2021 be kept in abeyance.

16

Custodial Torture Challenges Democracy and Dignity[1]

Torture leaves behind for its victims a suffocating penitentiary in which one's inner scream becomes deafening, deadening…

– Maria Popova

1. The *Tribune*, 18 January 2024; *Punjabi Tribune*. 23 January 2024.

The prime minister's recent advice earlier this month to the top brass of the police establishment to shun danda, along with his declaration that the new criminal laws have been crafted with the spirit of "citizen first, dignity first and justice first", is a hopeful augury for the much-delayed enactment of a comprehensive, standalone legislation to prevent recurring acts of custodial torture that shame the nation. The New Year should indeed be an occasion for the country to reinforce its democratic credentials, anchored in a steadfast commitment to the advancement of human dignity as the foremost fundamental right.

The much-awaited comprehensive legislation addressing various aspects of the crime of torture will be in furtherance of the guaranteed right to life with dignity under Article 21. Such a law will also enable India to ratify the United Nations Convention against Torture (UNCAT), which has not been possible in the absence of a compliant domestic law, despite India being a signatory to the Convention as early as 1977. India's ratification of the UNCAT will spare the country the embarrassment of facing repeated calls for accountability at the United Nations Human Rights review meetings, for non-ratification of the Convention. Ironically, in the first resolution to be proposed by a third-world country, it was India that had initiated the United Nations Resolution 32/64 of 8 December 1977, calling upon governments to unilaterally comply with the declaration against torture. Over the years, India has been a signatory to several international treaties that prohibit torture in any form and seek its elimination. Articles 51(c) and 253 of the Indian Constitution mandate respect for international law and compliance therewith. Considering its legitimate aspiration for a rightful role in shaping the new world order anchored in democracy and respect for human rights, India cannot be seen standing with the likes of Angola, Bahamas, Brunei, Gambia, Haiti, Palau and Sudan, who have not ratified the UNCAT.

Pertinently, the necessity of a standalone comprehensive legislation, covering several aspects connected with custodial torture, has been recognised by a Select Committee of Parliament, which had, in a demonstration of bipartisan support, recommended such a law in the form of the Prevention of Torture bill, 2010. Regrettably, fourteen years hence, the nation still awaits this critical piece of legislation against torture. The Law Commission of India in its 273rd Report

(2017), and the National Human Rights Commission, in an affidavit filed before the Supreme Court, have also endorsed the advisability of such legislation. The need for a comprehensive anti-custodial law, on the lines of UNCAT, as against a piecemeal tinkering with the wholly inadequate provisions in the existing criminal laws to address several issues arising out of the acts of custodial torture is self-evident. These include: a comprehensive definition of torture as a specified crime; prosecution of delinquent public servants including police authorities; mode and manner of lodging of complaints against custodial torture; protection of public officials against vexatious complaints; ensuring fair and impartial investigation; the question of burden of proof; interim compensation and rehabilitation of victims and witnesses of custodial torture; parameters for deciding the quantum of compensation to be awarded to victims; speedy trial and disposal of complaints; grievance redressal mechanism for complaints that may arise from such trials and disposal thereof; protection of victims, witnesses and complainants; education and sensitization of police authorities and public servants to encourage the use of scientific methods for effective and timely investigation and interrogation. Endorsing the need for legislation as an instrument of policy, the Consultative Council of European Judges (CCJE), stated in its Opinion no. 18 (2015): "A lack of legislation … may be contrary to the principle of legal certainty." The enactment of requisite legislation, apart from reinforcing the nation's commitment to constitutionalism and democracy, will disable fugitives from the law, currently abroad, from evading justice in India based on apprehension of torture in custody.

Torture is a crime that scars the soul, mutilates the body, breaks human will and dehumanises the victim. It leaves behind for its victims, as author Maria Popova has said, "a suffocating penitentiary in which one's inner scream becomes deafening, deadening…", and the deepest sense of alienation in one's innermost recesses, "cold as ice and heavy as a stone…" There is no scope, therefore, for executive apathy, legislative lassitude and judicial inconsistency/ambivalence in the matter of a joint resolve against torture, anywhere and in any form. The enactment of anti-torture legislation is a collective burden of the executive, legislative and judicial wings of the Indian state, who are mandated by the first principles of constitutional governance to work in unison for the advancement of national goals.

With our debilitating politics generally limited to a constant "jostling in the crowd" over personal vanities and political animosities, the representatives of the people cannot escape their share of responsibility for ignoring the compelling priority of our times. Nor has the highest constitutional Court been able to effectively fill a glaring gap in the law and ensure the effectuation of its elevating jurisprudence on human dignity in relation to acts of torture. The landmark judgments of the Court in this regard that demand validation through a purposive, effective implementation include Sunil Batra (2017); Francis Coralie Mullin (1981); D.K. Basu (1997); Prithpal Singh (2012); Shabnam (2015); K.S. Puttaswamy (2017); Nambi Narayanan (2018); Romila Thapar (2018).

Indisputably, a nation inspired by the ideals of a dignitarian Constitution cannot carry the burden of an unconscionable indifference to the inadequacy of legal structures to prevent brazen infractions of individual dignity by torture in the custody of the state's agencies. India's pre-eminence in the global arena will rest on the strength of its democratic edifice, sustained and nurtured by an abiding deference to human rights and accountability of state power. For all the above reasons and more, the logic of an effective anti-torture legislation is unexceptionable. The question is: will keepers of the constitutional faith vindicate the republic's conscience? The resilience of a nation on the move will be tested by whether those responsible for charting the nation's destiny and revitalising its democracy live up to their responsibilities.

17

A Test of Governance[1]

The ultimate test of elections is whether they express the muffled sighs of the oppressed, yearning for a life of dignity.

1. The *Tribune*, 6 November 2024.

In a never-ending "festival of democracy", another round of elections has been announced, including the four by-elections to the Punjab Vidhan Sabha. Clearly, much is at stake in these elections for the Bhagwant Mann government. An electoral reverse in the bypolls after its disappointing performance in Haryana could demoralise the ruling party's cadres and raise doubts about its future. The government's immediate challenge, therefore, is to demonstrate its political dominance in the state by winning the by-elections. Midway into its present tenure, its real test will be a little over two years from now, at the end of the government's present term, when its performance will be judged on the touchstone of a demonstrably just governance that can address the grave challenges faced by the state.

The land of the gurus and the five rivers, known as the granary of India and the sword arm of the nation, finds its people in distress. The hopelessness of the marginalised masses crushed by penury and the resultant loss of dignity, rampant drug addiction, large-scale migration of the unemployed youth to foreign lands in search of an elusive future, administrative malfeasance and the widening social divide, heightened by unconscionable economic disparities, have scarred the soul of Punjab. An understaffed constabulary tasked to address the stirrings of radicalism, political violence, gangsterism and a perpetual face-off between government and the dominant farming community over several issues, the latest being the stubble-burning cases and delayed paddy procurement, together with a continuing slide in several development indices, presents a depressing story of a state in decline. A look at the Niti Aayog's Sustainable Development Goal (SDG) rankings for Punjab for 2023-24 confirms this harsh, irrefutable reality. For instance, on SDG-8 related to Decent Work and Economic Growth, Punjab, which was once among the nation's top three states on most development parameters, is now ranked at number 18. On Gender Equality (SDG-5), it is ranked at number 19, and is at number 8 for Good Health and Well-being (SDG-3). On account of the fiscal profligacy of successive governments, the state's debt burden is more than Rs 3.51 lakh crores as of March 2024 (India Policy Forum, 2024, Economic Development of Punjab, India Prospects and Policies). According to the Niti Aayog's Multidimensional Poverty Index for 2023, 4.75 per cent of Punjab's population lives below the Multidimensional Poverty Index.

All political parties must share responsibility for this situation. Self-serving certificates of progress and development by successive ruling dispensations only attest the hypocrisy of our politics. The renewal of the state demands a cooperative endeavour based on cooperation between stakeholders and premised upon a broad democratic consensus on the way forward, for which a necessary first condition is the eschewing of politics of vendetta against political rivals. To rescue Punjab from the vicious cycle of economic stagnation and galloping unemployment, the AAP government, with its unprecedented legislative majority, is expected to take sound policy decisions to secure the state's future. It could start with fine-tuning of its agricultural policy, including crop diversification and rationalisation of water consumption, given the precarious water situation in the state, both in terms of its quality and future availability. A report by the Global Commission on the Economics of Water, released in October 2024, has drawn attention to the link between unsustainable subsidies and the imprudent water use for agriculture in India. The diminishing availability of potable water in several districts of Punjab and frightening forecasts in this regard present an existentialist crisis. The state's education and health sectors need a transformational revisiting for reasons recorded in several official documents.

Above all, it is time to recognise that no government can rest its claim to popular support solely on the basis of unsustainable freebies and state largesse, simply because no leader or political party can command an economic impossibility. The irrefutable logic of the law of diminishing returns compels a qualitative change in the practice of our politics. Political parties cannot remain captive to the pull of power regardless of the ends to which it is applied. Nor can competitive politics regress to a point where public discourse is constantly debased by reckless personal accusations against political opponents without a meaningful conversation around the grave challenges we face.

The Bhagwant Mann government has the time and opportunity still to deliver upon its promises and to vindicate its much-asserted claim of being a government with a difference. And, in its endeavours to pull the state out of the morass in which it finds itself, it is entitled to support from the Central government in the best traditions of cooperative federalism. Also, the government must trust the electorate with the truth of the situation and engage constructively with the Opposition with a view to forging a meaningful consensus on the way forward, while allowing for ideological contestation and the pursuit of political ambitions. The Opposition, on its part, should accept responsibility for facilitating the right policy choices in the larger interests of the state. Can we hope for a truly participatory and enlightened political engagement around the defining imperatives of our times in the ensuing elections?

And all parties, particularly the Congress, which is in a revanchist mode in the state, will do well to remember the unmistakable message of recent elections in the neighbouring states, that the collective wisdom of the people shaped by the memories of their lived experiences manifests itself eventually and owes no apology to the predictions of political pundits. The ultimate test of elections in the deepening of democracy is whether they yield leaders and policies that command the people's trust and give expression to the muffled sighs of the oppressed, yearning for a life of dignity. The by-elections in Punjab will indeed test our ability to take electoral democracy beyond momentary impulses and transient passions, to the realisation of its higher purposes.

18

Liberalism: Pulsating and Vibrant[1]

Though in retreat, we want our liberalism to be pulsating and vibrant.

1. *Indian Express* (8 April 2017; extracted from 'A Hope in a Challenged Democracy: An Indian Narrative' (2020)

Brexit and the Trump presidency represent a silent revolution that shook the world, rejecting the unaddressed inequities and unfulfilled promises of liberal democracies and globalisation. BJP's ascendancy to power in May 2014 is seen as our own silent revolution against the established political order. It is a clear mandate in favour of decisive leadership and against the status quo, mounted on an offer of hope for the people in their future. Thankfully, the mandate is not seen as a vote to deface, defile and disown the ideals we stand for. In these challenging times, we need to elevate our politics that can measure up to the enormity of the task.

The nation demands leadership that is daring and humble, caring and wise, such that it can summon the national will to foster national renewal. In an "era of churn", our ability to "nourish selfhood without selflessness", "individuality without individualism" is on test. Quite clearly, we need to forge a new social compact that would resist "...the poison of majoritarianism and the intimidation of ultra nationalism" (Pratap Bhanu

Mehta). For this, we need leadership powered by selflessness and vision that mirrors our yearning for a just social order based on freedom and inclusion.

In the infancy of our existence as a free nation, we were privileged to be guided by tall men and women whose lives were a saga of sacrifice in the cause of freedom and who defined its value for us. Somewhere along the journey, we lost our way when the pursuit of power as an end in itself became the principal obsession of political parties and their leaders, signalling the demise of ideology and the contest of ideas. In the process, small, scheming and timid "leaders" who confuse power for authority and think nothing of sacrificing principle for power rose in the hierarchy of their respective parties, suborning the institutions of governance and diminishing the credibility of the political system in the process. To redeem our tryst with destiny, we are obliged to reclaim our liberal legacy by locating the larger purposes of politics in the dignity and esteem of our people. We have sustained our plurality despite its challenges.

We have defied the "tyranny of homogeneity", carrying in our hearts a vision in which all our people can travel together so that we may travel far. We are proud of a nation that rejoices in freedom as an "unending frenzy", values it over identity and is anchored in a liberal core. Though in retreat, we want our liberalism to be pulsating and vibrant.

19

The World in Conflict: A Failure of Leadership[1]

1. The *Hindu* (8 July 2025). This piece summarises the qualities of leadership and may be read with the eulogies reproduced in Appendix IV; *Lokmat* (English and Hindi) on 17 July 2025 and in Marathi on 18 July 2025.

In an era of global conflicts and democratic decline, the question of political leadership in the democratic world has acquired a heightened significance. Intensified rivalries in several parts of the world represent a failure of leadership. The unconscionable ambivalence of world leaders in standing up for principle over expediency and their abject surrender to hegemonic power speaks for itself. The tragedies of Ukraine, Gaza and the Israel-Iran conflict are a soul-scarring saga of the ravages of war caused by the insolence of power, untamed by humanitarian interdicts.

A conflict-driven world has demonstrated the moral bankruptcy of leaders who have accepted "the fixed realities of the world" and its "failing assumptions" without the moral compass to fix its degrading aberrations. Despite the fragile ceasefire between Israel and Iran brokered by US President Donald J. Trump from a position of overarching military superiority, the footprints of these hostilities will remain visible symbols of an oppressive exercise of military power that has taken thousands of innocent lives. Those responsible for the catastrophe have clearly forgotten the abiding lesson of history that people carrying a festering wound in their souls find closure only when injustice is avenged. Lasting peace in West Asia will remain hostage to an indelible sense of injustice and moral outrage.

It is, therefore, imperative to foster leadership that values justice above raw power and refuses to succumb to its seductions. In the deeply distressing trans-border conflicts that have driven the world perilously close to a global war, the moral and intellectual impoverishment of the principal actors has raised concerns about the failure of contemporary democracies to yield inspiring leadership, answerable to the "injunctions of conscience". The pretence of a functional rules-based international order helmed by the United Nations Charter stands demolished yet again, reconfirming the impotence of international law in outlawing the use of force in relations between nations. The illegal invasion of Iraq and parts of Ukraine are no more than footnotes of history.

But there are lessons to be learnt. The world needs leadership, driven by a search for global consensus and subject to the discipline of international law to address the defining challenges of our times, including the settlement of territorial disputes. This is a particularly important reminder for those who claim to lead the democratic world and propound the necessity of a credible international legal order.

Democratic leadership is about walking alone in defence of principle, where necessary. It is about holding on to the truth against all odds and about empowering the weak, giving them voice and agency. It is about uniting people in trying times and advancing human dignity by removing unconscionable disparities. Inspirational leadership is about an unremitting endeavour to create favourable conditions of social and political existence that can optimise the realisation of human potential in an environment of peace and harmony. And as shown in the tortious process of securing a fragile truce between Israel and Iran, deceit and two-facedness annul leadership.

Leadership does not emerge out of a vacuum. The convergence of "man, the moment and the place" produces leadership. And as Karl Marx reminded us famously, "Men make their own history, but they do not make it as they please ... (they do so) under circumstances existing already, given and transmitted from the past." The French statesman Chateaubriand proclaimed that "the leader of the nation must be the leader of the times", so that his exertions mirror the aspirations of the people, investing politics with a moral purpose larger than himself. The global conflicts in these times present an opportunity for democracies to look inwards for correction and to reinforce their appeal.

Indian democracy, which has survived several vicissitudes and a "thousand mutinies", has been enriched by the exertions and selflessness of several of its towering leaders, led by Mahatma Gandhi, who defined for us the meaning of transformative leadership. The Mahatma's promise of politics, impervious to the trappings of power and rooted instead in the moral imagination of the people yearning for freedom and dignity, enabled him to forge a sustainable non-violent struggle against injustice. He accomplished the "will of his age", defined it for the people, and personified it.

As a proud inheritor of the Gandhian legacy of morality-driven politics and drawing strength from its civilisational ethos of *Vasudhaiva Kutumbakam*, India must stand out in defence of justice everywhere. It must flex its moral muscle for shaping a just world order. Its economic heft, nuclear capabilities, and regional power status should enable India to espouse international morality without compromising its strategic autonomy or alienating key allies. In these defying times, we must summon our tallest leaders to collectively energise Indian democracy by establishing the exceptionality of their leadership "not for their pettiness or capacity to disappoint", but by a soaring vision in the service of national goals and global peace.

Our leaders must "reinforce the tone of modesty", introduce dignity at the centre of political processes, revive the spirit of collegiality, be seen as symbols of hope in times of "fracture and fear" and repurpose their politics beyond the pursuit of raw power. At this juncture of the nation's history, when domestic and external challenges threaten the social accord and disruptive shifts in the power pendulum are testing the societal equilibrium, we need leadership that is strong and compassionate, resolute but conciliatory, and decisive while striving for democratic consensus on critical issues.

Learning our lessons from the raging conflicts and injustices we must address, let us light our candles for the changemakers who survive in our memories as heroes long after their exit. For them, Thomas Carlyle, the essayist and historian, had said, "… the history of what man has accomplished in this world is at bottom the history of the Great Men who have worked here."[2]

2. Eulogies in Appendix IV carry inspiring illustrations of democratic leadership.

20

A Just Equilibrium

The upcoming hearing in the Supreme Court of the Presidential Reference arising out of the Court's judgment in the State of Tamil Nadu v. The Governor of Tamil Nadu (April 2025) is of seminal constitutional significance. This is because of the perceived encroachment of the state's defined sovereign functions and the troubling non-observance of conventional discipline in the exercise of high constitutional power. The advisory opinion of the Court, though not binding, will have significant persuasive value for the exercise of sovereign power by the states and the central government in the future.

In its adjudicatory decision, the Court has indicted the Tamil Nadu governor for withholding assent to the bills passed by the legislative assembly for an unreasonably long time. It held that the conduct of the governor was unconstitutional, and it was permissible for the Court to read into the silences of the Constitution an implicit obligation on the part of the governor to exercise constitutional discretion reasonably and impartially. Relying upon government circulars, the Court held that the decision by the governor and President concerning assent to legislative bills is required to be taken within three months from the date of the receipt of the government's recommendation for assent.

The judgment is unexceptionable for its constitutional logic as far as the conduct of the governor is concerned. However, the extension of the Court's reasoning to the exercise of presidential prerogatives and its suggestion to the President to seek the Court's advisory opinion "when deciding on Bills reserved by the Governor" is fraught and open to interrogation for judicial overreach. This is because the President's prerogatives were not directly in question before the Court and because the President's sovereign power operates in a different realm and on a different plane in our constitutional scheme. As repository of the highest sovereign power, the President is entitled to the fullest presumption of regularity in the performance of constitutional duties, unaffected by the assumed possibility of an irregular exercise of power. Inspired by national imperatives generally not amenable to judicially manageable standards, the nature of the President's functions places the head of state in a unique position that does not warrant equivalence with the governor, who holds office at the pleasure of the President as her representative in the state. It is not surprising, therefore, that in what is a clear disapproval of the Court's judgment, the President has sought the

Court's advisory opinion on the key constitutional issues that emanate from its decision.

The core question raised in the reference concerns the "constitutional boundaries of executive and judicial authority", which is fundamental to the republic's constitutional arrangement. Pertinently, because the advisory opinion of the Court cannot displace a binding judicial precedent, the reference is seen as an opening for a review of the judgment or justification for a possible legislative initiative to insulate the President from the restraints imposed by the Court, should the advisory opinion be at variance with the ratio and reasoning in the Tamil Nadu case, in so far as it relates to the President?

The reference also seeks the Court's view on several specific and substantial questions of public importance. These include whether "...the judiciary can modify or override constitutional powers exercised by the President or governor through Article 142" that confers upon the Supreme Court, judicial power of the widest amplitude. Despite its internal coherence and unimpeachable logic in relation to the conduct of the governor, the Court's decision can be questioned for its directions (cloaked as a suggestion) to the President to seek her advice under Article 143 of the Constitution on legal issues impinging on the legality of the legislative bills requiring Presidential assent. This has been critiqued, not unreasonably, as an unwarranted judicial intervention in the exercise of sovereign discretion, not necessitated by the scope of the legal challenge that was limited to the conduct of the governor of Tamil Nadu. This part of the judgment can also be faulted in view of the established processes of decision-making by the President, including those pertaining to legal counsel.

Judicial intervention in policy choices of the government/Parliament and in the exercise of sovereign power, unless palpably mala fide, has raised questions about the balance of constitutional power. The necessity of restraint in the exercise of judicial power has been reiterated by the Court in the Tamil Nadu case itself, holding that (In) "the exercise of self-imposed restraint … courts do not venture into areas of governance in which the Constitution gives a prerogative solely to the executive". Chief Justice Gavai, in his recent address at the Oxford Union, is reported to have endorsed a balanced exercise of judicial power.

Judges, made wise by experience, disciplined by law and elevated by knowledge, are expected to weigh and balance competing values, a function central to their role. The nation trusts the sagacity of the highest court to configure a just constitutional equilibrium of power so that the country's democratic order is not held hostage to the unfettered impulses of any single branch of the Indian state. As the nation's conscience-keeper, the Court is expected to vindicate this trust by the consistency and moral integrity of its judgments and by guarding against the "juridification of politics and politicisation of the judiciary". We know that it is in the wisdom of the wise that enduring answers to some of the vexed questions of our time will be found.

APPENDIX : I

Conversing Democracy and Dignity[1]

1. Edited conversation between Jyoti Malhotra and Dr Ashwani Kumar on the occasion of the launch of the latter's book *A Democracy in Retreat: Revisiting the Ends of Power* (2023) on 20 December 2023.

Jyoti Malhotra: Thank you so much, ladies and gentlemen, for coming here this evening. Your presence, no doubt, is a measure of the affection, admiration, and support for Dr Ashwani Kumar. But it's not just that. I do want to say here that the reason your presence is really important is because it is a vindication of your engagement with the ideas expressed in this book, *A Democracy in Retreat: Revisiting the Ends of Power.* We have been a republic for 74 years. Our Constitution gave India, us Indians, the rights and privileges of being a secular democratic republic. But 74 years on, is our democracy in retreat? What indeed is the relationship between democracy and power? Is there a limit to the exercise of power in a democracy? And if the answer to that is yes or no, as some may believe, who is going to draw these red lines? But without much further ado, I would like to start this conversation with Dr Ashwani Kumar.

Ashwani-ji, there are several abiding themes in this book. And the first one, of course, is about democracy and the democratic deficit that you talk about. You talk about certain authoritarian trends that have crept up in our democracy. But tell us a little bit more about what you mean by that.

Ashwani Kumar: Well, I think there is a context to the book and to the themes that I have chosen. In 2016, when my term in the Rajya Sabha came to an end, after a long and satisfying period in parliament, I thought to myself that there had to be a larger purpose to life. I have been the law minister. That is the highest one could go in the profession. I have been a parliamentarian for 14 years, chaired important parliamentary committees, and was entrusted by the prime minister to be his special envoy to Japan. Almost everything that I could have wanted in life or desired for myself was achieved. And I said to myself that for the remaining part of my life, I must have a purpose larger than the appellations of authority. What could that purpose be? And there was absolutely no doubt in my mind that the larger public purpose of life, and certainly for someone in public life, should be the advancement of human dignity. That is why I wrote my first book on this subject, titled *Human Dignity, a Purpose in Perpetuity*. The present book is a continuation or a sequel to the thoughts that I had expressed in that book.

When I talk about democracy, its relationship to power is, of course, a given. But what I had in mind was the relationship of democracy to dignity. Democracy is premised on inclusion, on fairness, on the rule of law, on justice, not on seclusion, not on exclusion. And it is premised first and foremost on equality, which gives us dignity and which we share in common with all our citizens. So, democracy and dignity are interchangeable. Why? Because the promise of democracy, if fulfilled, inevitably promotes human dignity. So, in every country, in every situation, where you see human dignity at a discount, you can immediately infer that democracy is in decline in that country and vice versa. And, therefore, the collection of articles in this book has one strand that runs throughout; that is, the challenges to human dignity, and therefore, challenges to democracy.

Jyoti Malhotra: But these disturbing trends you talk about in the functioning of our republican democracy today, for example, the exercise of arbitrary power. Can you elaborate on these?

Ashwani Kumar: Yes. There are examples galore of the arbitrary exercise of power. This is writ large in so many things that we are witnessing today. For example, the expulsion of members of Parliament. This is, in my view, a clear case of the exercise of power in an arbitrary manner. I can understand that you can hide behind a rule, and I can understand that you can hide behind the plenary power of an institution. But the point is that a constitutional democracy is premised on a benign exercise of power. The existence of power is one thing. Its exercise is completely another. What legitimises power is the manner of its exercise, and that is why we keep repeating this day in and day out, whether somebody acknowledges its reality or not, its truth or not. We are not only a majoritarian democracy. We are a constitutional democracy. That is why the theme that runs throughout the book and the related themes are about the accountability of power. To whom? Not to A or B but to the discipline and spirit of the Constitution. The moment we see that spirit being violated, we know that our constitutional democracy needs protection.

Jyoti Malhotra: Now, clearly, you are an avowed constitutionalist. I mean, that's very clear from your writings, not just in this book but otherwise as well. And yet, you don't give the Supreme Court, the Honourable Supreme Court, 10 out of 10 in its defence of the republic. Why is that? Why do you think that the record of the judiciary is mixed?

Ashwani Kumar: I am very pained to accept that reality. I have worshipped two gods. One is God above me, and the other is the courts where I've spent all my life. And, it has been my ambition, as Chief Justice Thakur would tell you, to be the Chief Justice of India. But that could not be. And the reason why, at one point in time, in 1986, when I was given an offer to become a High Court judge, I declined. Only because by that time, I had realised that judges were so powerless, they cannot even defend themselves when all kinds of hurtful innuendos are hurled against them because of their judgments or otherwise. But the record of the honourable Supreme Court, by and large, I would say, has been stellar, in the sense that the Supreme Court and higher judiciary have earned respect and acceptability in the minds of the people, and it is not for nothing. These courts have, at different points in time, come out with very profound judgments. I mean, Puttaswamy, Shreya Singhal, Navtej Johar, all these judgments are outstanding.

But my problem with the Court is that it does not enforce its own lofty edicts. And that is what Chief Justice Chandrachud himself has said in one of his judgments, that the point is to enforce the edicts. Now, who is to enforce these? Also, one or two judgments during the time of the pandemic were very disappointing. But another judgment, and the one authored by Justice Chandrachud on the vaccination policy, was outstanding. So, no institution is perfect. The record of the Supreme Court is certainly a mixed record. And in terms of defending the liberties of people, its record in recent years has not been very elevating. And I am very, very pained to say this, because for me, the Supreme Court is a venerable institution and I will always regard it as a venerable institution. But the truth is that some of its judgments have been very disappointing. And I would also say that some of its judgments on its own power and the way it has exercised its judicial review power, is a classic case in the exercise of stretched constitutionalism.

For example, the Court virtually rewrites the Constitution in the appointment of Election Commissioners case. I know that the popular view is in favour of the judgment, or could be in favour of the judgment. But as a constitutionalist, I don't agree with that judgment at all. Its premises are flawed. It amounts to virtually rewriting the Constitution against the will of Parliament, and it brings the Court into conflict with another great institution of democracy. After all, we can't forget, whatever the aberrations may be, that Parliament, as representative of the will of the people, is the supreme democratic institution. I am not saying that Parliament can't go wrong or that parliamentarians don't go wrong, but for that matter, judges are also not infallible. They also go wrong. And that is proved by the fact that so many of the Supreme Court judgments have been corrected by the Supreme Court itself at a given point in time, deferring to the wisdom of a future day. So, I think, the great glory of the Supreme Court as an institution has been that to a very large extent, it has kept hope with the people.

But it has also faltered. And when it falters and when the aberrations speak through judicial decisions, they are enlarged, because the Supreme Court is supposed to be the ultimate guardian of the Constitution, even though I don't agree with that. I have said in my book that democracy is secure eventually only in the assertion of the people through mass mobilisation helmed by leaders who can rise above themselves.

Jyoti Malhotra: Justice Lokur is smiling at your observations. But I do want to draw the attention of the audience to another very interesting theme in your book, which is that it's not always possible to lay the blame at the door of the ruling party or the regime in power. And you talk about the citizenry, people like us, like you and me, like all of us in this room. And what is it about us? What is it about our responsibility to stand up to this arbitrary exercise of power, if you like? What is the responsibility of the citizens, our role, our duties?

Ashwani Kumar: I must answer this by telling you about a true conversation, a brief three-minute-four-minute conversation that I had with the late Shrimati Indira Gandhi when I was just beginning my career. This was immediately around the time of the Emergency. Around that time in 1975-76, I had gone to meet her as part of a group of lawyers, and for some reason, I stayed back, and she gave me a private audience for two or three minutes. And she asked me, "Ashwani, what is happening in the courts?" Those were the Emergency days. There was a lot of resentment against the Congress party. And I said, '*Madam, Courts mein to mahaul theek nahin hain, log emergency ke khilaf hain; intelligentsia hum se door jaa raha hai, humko intelligentsia ko apne nazdeek karna chahiye.*'

She pondered for a moment and said that it was not derogatory. It was exactly how she felt, what her experiences were. Mrs Indira Gandhi was never derogatory to anyone. She said, "You talk about the intelligentsia, who don't even go to vote." And I had no answer to that. It is true. When Dr Manmohan Singh contested an election, Smt. Phoolan Devi won. Dr Manmohan Singh lost. I was in charge of one of the voting booths in Friends Colony, where there were about 300 voters. By 3 p.m., only eighty people had turned up to vote. And out of those eighty, 20-30 would have voted for somebody else. This was his logical constituency, even though those voters did not come out to vote.

Therefore, there is a failure, a collective failure on all our parts. People who think they know don't walk the talk. The challenge is to walk the talk. People who talk of dignity must be willing to pay the price for their dignity. You can't defend somebody else's dignity if you can't defend your own. And therefore, at some point in time, not only in India, but in most democracies of the world, the affluent and the intelligent somehow seem to have become irrelevant in the political processes, in the electoral processes of democracy. They may help in creating a consciousness, as we all try to do when we write. But the change will only come through massive political assertion and mobilisation. And I repeat, by leaders who can rise above themselves. So, the challenge is to find those few people who can show the way. "*Nishan-e-raah dikhate the jo sitaaron ko; bhatak rahe hain kisi mard-e-raah-daan ke liye. Jo quamein, jo log sitaaron ko bhi raasta dikhate the, hum jaise, Hindustan ke log, aaj bhatak rahe hain kisi raah-daan ke liye.*"

About human dignity, Iqbal wrote, "*Na tu zameen ke liye hai, na aasma ke liye, jahan hain tere liye, tu nahin jahan ke liye.*" God has created the world for man, not man for the world. *Aur usi ka doosra band hai, "nishan-e-raah dikhate the jo sitaaron ko bhatak rahe hain kisi mard-e-raah-daan ke liye*".

Jyoti Malhotra: You know, I am going to come to the question of leadership in a second, but I do want to press you on the role of the citizenry. Now, 143 members of Parliament have been suspended in the last few days, the highest ever in the history of our republic, of our democracy. And it's still counting. And by the way, Manoj Jha was most eloquent when he announced in front of the press, and of course outside Parliament, when he said, "I am suspended." And I think he wears it as a badge of honour. But the question to you, Ashwani-ji, is that 143 members of Parliament have been suspended. You would have thought that people would be out in the streets. You would have thought that political parties would lead protests, and be out on the streets, not just in Delhi, but across the country. Why do you think this hasn't happened, or it's not happening?

Ashwani Kumar: We, as a nation, are a very tolerant people. You know, we wait till things really reach a point where there is no way out. But I do believe that this episode has caught the attention of the people. And I think people will absorb it. But again, public memory is short. To keep these aberrations alive in the public mind is a function of communication. It is a function of leadership. Who will communicate what, when, and how? You can't speak of Harold Laski and Habermas to the ordinary people of the country.

But of course, you can summarise their thoughts in a manner that touches their heart.

The chapter on "Poetic Dignity in Public Discourse" is all about how, during the days of the freedom movement, people like Josh Malihabadi, Akbar Allahabadi, and all such people galvanised the nation through their poetry, through their articulation—understated, elegant, refined, not coarsened by calumny and personalised vicious discourse. They said the right thing, in the right language to the right audience, at the right time. And it had an appeal much beyond hundreds of these books that could be written and read.

Therefore, the challenge of leadership today and the challenge of political parties, if I may say so, is to find in their ranks leaders who can set a narrative for this country. One narrative for the country has been set, we all know. The alternative narrative is floundering somewhere in the air. We say ten different things at ten different times. I want to say that the Opposition certainly has a right in a democracy to oppose, expose and depose. But the Opposition also cannot claim moral superiority and intellectual superiority of judgment in all matters. It was wrong for the Opposition to condemn the government during the time of the pandemic. Completely wrong. It is wrong, for example, for the Opposition to find small holes here and there in foreign policy or on defence-related matters. Maybe one's view is different. I would have done it differently, had I been the foreign minister. But when it comes to weighty issues of national security, weighty issues of foreign policy, you have to defer to the judgment of the government of the day. It may be any government. It could be A, B, C, or D.

I remember during the Kargil War, I was a spokesperson of the Congress party. And I remember one of my colleagues, I won't name him, was very critical of PM Vajpayee. I went to Mrs Gandhi and said, "Madam, this is not sounding right. We are finding fault with the prime minister of a country which is at war." She said, "I agree with you, I have told these people so many times not to say these things, but they don't listen to me. And the next day, the damage was done."

Therefore, life must gravitate towards moderation. Democracy is about moderated politics. Constructive politics, by definition, is moderated politics. If you don't gravitate towards moderation, you will get the plot wrong. You cannot get it right. Even now, I am saying, the country is looking to 2024. To get an alternative narrative on the ground and running is the challenge of the Opposition leadership. It is not for us to decide. I hope something will happen, but that's the challenge.

Jyoti Malhotra: So, you also talk about the need to reach out to the Opposition, for example, or the need to reach out to people who don't agree with you. So in a sense, this language of our public life, whether it is in Parliament or outside, and the coarsening of our public discourse, you refer to, of course, in Chapter XXXIII in the book, which talks about dignity in public discourse. I think just the general coarsening of our public language, whether it's on the part of the BJP or on the part of the Congress, is something that we all decry, but tell us how this impacts the life of a democracy.

Ashwani Kumar: You know, the worst thing that you can do for democracy is for political parties and their leaders to call each other names. You know, *humare yahan ki ek sanskriti rahi hai ki andhe ko andha nahin kehte, Surdas kehte hain, andhe ko andha kahoge to usko chubh jaati hai yeh baat.* Ghalib said, "*Har ek baat pe kehte ho tum, ki tu kya hai; tumhi kaho ki ye andaaz e guftagoo kya hai.*" In every sentence, if you're going to be abusive of your opponent, treating your opponent as a personal enemy, what chance does democracy have? There's no chance! *Is hamam mein sabhi nange hain—koi ek party nahin hai jo ye claim kar sakti hai ki our discourse is very civilised.* No! Who provoked whom is another debate, but the point is that you can't fight certain people on their own turf. If you are claiming a qualitative distinction for your politics, you can't be in a competitive game of calumny. And the moment you fall into that trap, you are at the same level. Your distinction is defeated. That is why I say that the chapter I wrote, 'Poetic Dignity in Political Discourse', is important. I mean, every sentiment can be expressed in verse, or in elegant prose or speech. Do you have to abuse each other?

I remember with great pain in my heart, because Mr Rajiv Gandhi brought me into politics. I have the greatest respect for him. It was painful to hear things said about him during the Bofors controversy, but now we are saying the same thing about the PM. How does it make us better? Have we learned from history? No! People who refuse to learn from history are condemned by it. And therefore, a time has come when, in order to restore our cherished democracy to its strength, we need to rise above ourselves. We need to rise above our passions, our anger, our hurt. All of these are absolutely natural sentiments. You are bound to be hurt if you are told wrong things. But then to expect from those hurt, not to react, is also wrong. They will also react. Therefore, this unending spiral of venomous, coarsened political discourse is hollowing out the foundations of India's democracy. And that, Jyoti, is the challenge of leadership.

Jyoti Malhotra: So, what now?

Ashwani Kumar: What now is the last question? Well, *sitaron se aage jahan aur bhi hain, abhi ishq ke imtehaan aur bhi hain.* I don't know where life is going to take me. I said the same thing when Thakur Sahib released my two books. He has always done me the honour, and he's here today. I'm deeply grateful to him. I said at that point of time, "*Jab tak zindagi hai, jab tak safar hai, jab tak justuju hai, there's never a full stop.*" Where my destiny will take me, only God knows. But I do continue to believe that if God spares me some healthy years in the future, I will continue to be active in the public sphere. It may be in one form or the other. And I will try to spend more time doing things that I missed out on, which is reading more literature and less hard politics.

APPENDIX : II

National Judicial Appointments Commission, Judicial Review and Legislative Sovereignty[1]

1. Edited Interview of Dr Ashwani Kumar to PTI on 6 April 2025.

PTI: Justice Varma's episode has brought the issue of judicial accountability and judicial appointments into focus. Has the incident dented the image of the judiciary?

Ashwani Kumar: It is absolutely true that the unfortunate incident has cast a long shadow on the institutional integrity of the judiciary, but it has also given rise to many fundamental principles of constitutional jurisprudence. The fact is that in this particular case, even during the initial steps of the inquiry process, the judge stands pilloried and condemned both in the media and by virtue of a punitive transfer to Allahabad and the order of withdrawal of work from the judge. I think the time has come for the Supreme Court to review the in-house procedure to make it more just, to make it more balanced as to be able to subserve its purpose, which was to protect judges from frivolous allegations and, at the same time, to provide an effective redressal mechanism to address the issues that ail the judiciary.

PTI: You, being the former law minister and the original bill for the National Judicial Appointments Commission (NJAC) was also formulated during your tenure, do you think that the time has come for revisiting the NJAC, considering that there have been various voices emerging, including those from the Rajya Sabha, in this regard?

Ashwani Kumar: First of all, let me delink questions about Justice Varma's episode from the NJAC. The time for NJAC was right in 2014-15 when it was first mooted and put to a vote. It is certainly ripe today, and I am convinced that the processes of public opinion are moving robustly in favour of an alternative mechanism for the appointment of judges. It could be on the lines of NJAC, or it could be something better. And I tell you why I believe that the time for NJAC is here. I have a serious issue with the validity of the NJAC judgment, whereby the NJAC was struck down as unconstitutional. The principal reason for the Court to strike down the NJAC, in its wisdom, was that government representatives and eminent persons to be appointed by the government on the NJAC could compromise the independence of the judiciary.

In my considered view as a lawyer, and this is the view that the minority judgment of Justice Jasti Chelameswar takes in that case, there is no equivalence between the independence of the judiciary and the manner and mode of appointment of judges. To extend the doctrine of independence of the judiciary to the mode and manner of appointment of judges is a flawed extension of the doctrine. For example, from where do we draw the presumption that the government will always recommend judges who are not first class or that the judges will always select the best judges? Recent events have shown the reverse to be true. To date, some of the finest judges of the Indian Supreme Court and the high courts were appointed when the Government of India alone was the appointing authority. And some of the not very fine examples of judicial appointments have been seen after the collegium system came into being.

This is not to suggest that the collegium system consciously selects not the very best of judges, but it is certainly an argument to say that the weighty issues of judicial independence, which certainly should be, and is a part of the basic structure of the Constitution, could not be linked to the mode and manner of appointment of judges. And as has been said, for how long will the people have faith in judges who have lost faith in themselves and in their representatives? If you start drawing a wedge between the judiciary and executive in the matter of high judicial appointments, a day is not far off when there will be an institutional conflict, and that will be absolutely fatal for the governance in a constitutional democracy.

PTI: Now that the NJAC has already been struck down by the Court, do you agree with the assertion that the appointment mechanism impacts the independence of the judiciary even though Parliament, which has the supreme power to formulate laws, had brought the constitutional amendment, overwhelmingly approved by the members.

Ashwani Kumar: I have already stated that I don't believe that the NJAC, as proposed or contemplated for the future, with the government being represented by the law minister and some other people being appointed to the committee for the appointment of judges, will impact judicial independence. Quite the contrary, it will lead to more broad-based consultations. It will perhaps lead to better appointments. It is a flawed extension of the doctrine of judicial independence to suggest that in case the committee for appointment of judges has a government nominee or an executive representative on it, the independence of the judiciary will be impacted. Quite the contrary, I don't think that is true either in constitutional theory or in practice.

PTI: We have seen in the recent past that various laws passed by Parliament have ended up being challenged in the Courts. The latest case being the Waqf Law, which has just been passed by the Parliament, and it has already been challenged by various people and the One Nation One Election Bill is likely to be challenged, considering that there is a lot of opposition to it. What do you think about the issue of various laws being challenged again and again?

Ashwani Kumar: Well, this is a very pertinent question, and I think this is one of the principal issues that this nation and its political and judicial processes have to address in the very near future. We see that every major question of political significance and ramifications is somehow shunted off to the Supreme Court. It may suit the political executive of the time to have difficult questions being settled by the Supreme Court, or it may suit the Opposition to challenge every measure of the government in the Supreme Court, but this is unfair to the judiciary as an institution. The judiciary has itself repeatedly said that it is not a part of the judicial function to enter into the "political thicket", which means questions which are essentially political. And the Court has said that it neither has the mandate nor the means to determine such questions. These must eventually be determined in the people's court.

Therefore, when the judiciary sits in judgment over issues of great political moment, questions are being raised about whether the judiciary is unduly enlarging its remit. The power of judicial review, which was invested by the Constitution in the judiciary, was essentially meant to protect the citizens in the defence of their fundamental rights. It was not intended to be an instrument for the judiciary to nullify the will of the people. And please don't forget that when the 99th Constitutional Amendment that brought in the NJAC was struck down, it had the support of an overwhelming majority in Parliament. So, at some point in time, we have to ask, can you take away the majoritarian will of the people from the constitutional and democratic processes? You cannot! At the same time, we have to temper the sovereign will by principles of accountability enshrined in the Constitution. And that is the role with which the Supreme Court is charged, but the Supreme Court cannot use that role to progressively keep enlarging its own remit at the cost of Parliament's remit. So these questions are very pertinent and have to be addressed. You would have seen that voices are being raised inside Parliament that this can't go on.

APPENDIX : III

Address by the Author at the FRIDAY GROUP meeting of Supreme Court lawyers in the Supreme Court Bar Library (2018) on the broadening scope of "Judicial Review"

Thank you very much for giving me the singular honour of addressing you. I am hesitant to give a formal lecture to an audience as well-versed in constitutional law as all of you are. But I thought that I should speak to you on a subject which is of vital importance, not only in terms of our day-to-day understanding of the parameters of constitutional judicial review but also in the larger framework of the functioning of our parliamentary democracy.

I do believe, and I think it is necessary for me to emphasise that while judicial review has served an extremely important purpose in the functioning and evolution of our democracy and in the enlargement of a rights-based jurisprudential regime of which we are so proud, there is also lurking in the shadows a real possibility of an emerging conflict between the institutions of India's libertarian democracy. I have in mind the rising apprehension in the minds of the legislators and the executive about the enlarged judicial power vis-à-vis other organs of the state, namely, Parliament and the executive. Now, this is a perennial debate. It is not a debate which will conclude today, nor is it a debate which began today.

This has been an ongoing debate in almost all democracies, particularly constitutional democracies, where the sovereign power of the people, normally to be exercised by their representatives in parliament, elected by them and speaking through the executive, is also now regarded as not an absolute power, but a power tempered by certain constitutional norms, so that the normative factors in the exercise of sovereign power have now become the subject of jurisprudential and political discourse. It is a subject concerned with the future of parliamentary democracy, the nature of democratic power. So these are very, very large issues and since all of you are informed citizens of this country, much before you are lawyers, I thought it would be right to share my perspectives on this.

Let me start by giving you a historical perspective of how judicial review power came to be as extensive in the country today as it is. We all know that with the rise of PIL as an instrument of justice, as an instrument for ensuring access to justice, the court came to be seized with issues which normally would not have come to the Court. As conceived way back in 1987, this was an instrument conceived to subserve the purposes of the marginalised sections of society who were unable to enforce their constitutional freedoms and rights because of the lack of adequate resources, educational means and access to justice. That is how Justices Bhagwati and Krishna Iyer, in the heydays of their role on the Bench, carved out a special jurisdiction which has come to be known as epistolary jurisdiction. The Court's jurisdiction could be invoked even by a simple letter to the Court stating that fundamental rights of the marginalised are being trampled upon by the state or its instrumentalities and that the Court, as the ultimate arbiter of constitutional conscience, must ensure against the infraction of rights. However, over time, we saw this power taking on a colour, which I dare say was not in the contemplation of the framers of the Constitution. There are comparisons of India's judicial review power with the due process jurisprudence of the United States and the incompatibility doctrine in England, which has developed after the European Human Rights Act came to be introduced in the UK.

As we all know, there is a difference between the United Kingdom and India, which is governed by a written Constitution, unlike the United Kingdom. The conventions of the Constitution serve as the bedrock of a broader scheme within which parliamentary democracy functions.

Coming back to our own development of the doctrine of judicial review, it seems to be running in a direction which some political observers believe could bring the

Court into conflict with Parliament, and that's the last thing that India's constitutional democracy needs. This is the last thing that we, as people of India, need.

Parliament is relevant. It must always remain relevant because, at the end of the day, people speak through their representatives. It has been argued that the ills of democracy cannot give rise to judicial despotism, judicial supremacy or judicial excess, which is what judicial review has now come to appear to a very large number of people. I remember, and I would like to bring this to your attention, when I was the law minister and we were giving shape to the NJAC Bill, that was a time when the UPA government was not being allowed to function at all in Parliament. We could not get a single piece of legislation through because the Opposition insisted on disrupting Parliament and not having a meaningful debate on any bill. But there was one issue on which there was near unanimity, with the exception of Shri Ram Jethmalani. There was agreement that the NJAC (the Collegium System) in the present form must go, and the unfettered power of appointment of judges with the judiciary must go…

I had to steer that bill. I was convinced, as I am today, that the present collegium system alone, by itself, is no guarantee of judicial independence. Nobody has been accused of judicial non-independence when the ultimate power of appointment of judges is vested with the government alone.

And this was there till the first judge's case … So till then, some of the finest judges of India were appointed by the government, and nobody had any complaint about the independence of judges. These judges have laid the foundations of a largely credible and independent Indian Judiciary.

Then comes this bill. The entire Parliament unites to pass the NJAC Amendment Bill. Why? Because there is a lurking distrust amongst parliamentarians that their functions are being taken over by the Court.

If you ask the judges of the Supreme Court, they would probably disagree with that proposition because the argument in favour of a continuing enlargement of judicial review is that when the executive and Parliament fail to perform their functions, judges have no other option but to step in to uphold the constitutional conscience. The philosophical and jurisprudential basis of this argument is that judicial review, being mandated by the Constitution, is not anti-democratic because the Constitution is made by the people, and the people, through the Constitution, gave the power of judicial review to the judiciary. Therefore, it is not as if the brethren in the black robes are there to outdo the will of the parliamentarians.

It is because the Constitution itself envisages a separation of powers and the role of judicial adjudication or constitutional adjudication being entrusted entirely to the judiciary, judges exercise their constitutional function. This is the argument which is advanced by the judiciary. And to an extent, it is a correct argument. I have no quarrel with this argument. The difficulty arises when you have to set the boundaries of respective powers. Parliament cannot be allowed to curtail the non-negotiable fundamental freedoms and rights of any citizen. I am entirely in agreement with this proposition. And therefore, I think that judicial review is a necessary ingredient of our constitutional scheme. And that is why successive judicial decisions, and rightly so in my view, hold that judicial review is a part of the unalterable and non-negotiable basic structure of the constitution and that Parliament, even in the exercise of its constituent power, cannot be allowed to alter or tinker with fundamental and the non-negotiable human freedoms which need to be protected against the momentary impulses of transitory majorities. The argument that certain rights are inalienable because they are inherent in us as a human person, which Parliament, speaking on behalf of the people, cannot be allowed to tinker with, is the underlying philosophy of judicial review. Now, there is the question of determining the boundaries of power. In constitutional law, you will very often come across this phrase, "boundaries of power", meaning that different organs of the state must function within the boundaries of their power. Now, who will determine what the boundaries are? This is the function of the judiciary by the command of the Constitution under Articles 13, 32, Article 226, Article 136 and Article 142, which is mandated to be the arbiter of the limits of constitutional power.

Scholars have argued that harmonising of constitutional powers conferred on different organs of the state entails judicial self-restraint. Now, judicial self-restraint again is a doctrine that is not amenable to any set standard.

Please remember that the Court sits in several formations. Different judges may, and do, decide a particular set of facts differently because whenever there is an element of discretion, judges do not necessarily decide alike even on substantially similar facts. Therefore, since the Court does not sit *en banc*, that is, it doesn't sit together as a whole to decide a question of law, different judges of the Court decide the parameters of power and the banks of power differently. This issue is now in the realm of public discourse in the world's constitutional democracies and not only in India.

Constitutional scholars have written extensively on the subject and have argued that the inadequacies of the political system of parliamentary democracies and the inability of parliamentarians to hold to the faith that the people have imposed on them, is not to be answered by conferring an overriding power on judiciary—a coordinate branch of the government and that ultimately we need to have faith in the wisdom of the people. If a government and the representatives of the people are not delivering in the manner expected of them, they will be thrown out in the next election in the exercise of the sovereign will, reflected through a vote. But then, the contrary argument is that you can't wait for five years to check the aberrations; there must be some recourse. And that recourse in all constitutional democracies is with the Court.

However, if the power of judicial review is to remain meaningful and is not to be brought under assault by parliamentarians, it is absolutely necessary that the Courts recognise the limits of their power. Our Supreme Court nudged the government to bring a law on lynchings. A few months earlier, on my petition to nudge the Parliament to frame a law against custodial torture, the court dithered and baulked and held that since lawmaking is within the domain of Parliament and since the Attorney General has conceded that this is a valid demand, we think it is not necessary for us at this stage to interfere. Then, in Achyutanand's case, we see the Court giving directions under the Food and Safety Act for ensuring the purity of milk. In the AFSPA case, the Court engaged itself with the proportionate use of force by the army in a conflict zone.

I mean, people are asking whether the Court is competent to give these directions. At the same time, I would say that the Court's directions, particularly with regard to the socio-economic legislation, whether it relates to housing, shelter, education, health, environment, are extraordinarily commendable directions which go to serve the larger constitutional goals and human rights … So, the long and short of the discussion is that for any kind of limited power, and all power within our constitutional scheme is limited by the boundaries of the competing power, have to be harmonized so that no institution of state feels that there is an encroachment upon its domain as delineated in the constitutional scheme. Now, there is another problem with the argument of original intent.

There is no such thing as "original intent" when the Constitutions are supposed to be working over hundreds of years. And that is why it was people like Roscoe Pound, Judge Cardozo and others who said that Constitutions are meant to subserve the priorities, not of a decade, but for centuries. And therefore, it is inherent in the process of judicial and constitutional adjudication to tailor the Constitution to meet the demands of the present and future.

So, at the end of the day, I hope that this country will have parliamentarians who are wise, who are committed to upholding the trust that the people of India repose in them from time to time. And, I hope, we have judges who have no delusions of grandeur, exalted views of their own power and who recognise the limits which the constitutional scheme imposes on. I have no doubt that, on the whole, and by and large, we have outstanding judges who are true to their oath of office and try to do justice as best as they can.

And I do hope, in all our interests and in the interest of the nation, that the Court, Parliament and the executive function in tandem to deliver upon the promises made to the people of India on the eve of Independence, so that all of us, including the institutions of libertarian democracy, redeem their tryst with destiny.

Thank You!

APPENDIX : IV
Eulogies

Jawaharlal Nehru: A Legacy Carved into the Heart of History[1]

Nehru, who made history, remains alive in the thoughts of the nation

1. The *Tribune* (Online), 27 May 2025; *Punjabi Tribune*, 27 May 2025; *Punjab Kesari*, 26 May 2025; *Lokmat*, 27 May 2025; *Navodaya Times*, 27 May 2025; *Jagbani*, 27 May 2025

History, as Thomas Carlyle wrote, is shaped by extraordinary individuals—those who rise above personal ambition and dedicate their lives to the betterment of humankind. Endowed with courage, charisma, a will to succeed, and a passionate belief in the righteousness of their cause, such individuals leave an indelible imprint on the course of history. Jawaharlal Nehru, the iconic hero of India's freedom struggle and the nation's first prime minister, was one such towering figure.

The largeness of Nehru's vision has defined India's trajectory as a modern nation—one whose voice commands respect in the diplomatic corridors of the world. He envisioned India as a democratic state, governed by the rule of law and committed to secularism, inclusion, freedom, equality, dignity and justice for all. It fell to him as the nation's first prime minister to set in motion the process of realising the fundamental goals of the republic. Pandit-ji, as Nehru was affectionately addressed by his colleagues, believed that peace was the necessary first condition for India's progress and, therefore, steered clear of the Cold War rivalries, becoming at the same time a global ambassador of anti-colonialism and peacemaker of the world. It was his personal stature as a freedom fighter, humanist and a man of letters that ensured his place amongst the statesmen of his time. His initiatives in the field of science and technology have made possible India's status as a nuclear power, with a space programme that is the envy of the world. The establishment of the IITs and IIMs in the country is a tribute to his foresight. The Green and the White revolutions in India that have ensured the nation's food security are owed to Nehru's vision. And, a strong public sector was his instrument for achieving the nation's goal of self-reliance, a vision that has been vindicated.

The list of his accomplishments as prime minister and the excellence of his personality are part of the nation's folklore. But it was his selflessness, democratic temper and humility that endeared him to the multitude, whose affection was his greatest strength. Pure of heart, he reposed faith in those who proclaimed friendship and was not harsh even to those who were compulsively opposed to him. He recognised the right of conscientious dissent within his party and importance of the Opposition's role in a democracy, welcoming and even encouraging constructive opposition.

At a time when attempts are being made to deride and denounce his work, let it not be forgotten that memories of Pandit-ji's towering leadership cannot be obliterated by the propagandists. Those who wish to falsify history must know that truth is concrete and cannot be buried. It reinforces itself and finds utterance from time to time. Indeed, history cannot be willed, and Nehru, who made history, remains alive in the thought of the nation. His life of selflessness and sacrifice is an abiding testimony to his ennobling leadership. No rewriting of history can silence the deafening echo of his elevating humanism or the force of his thought. In these times of fracture and discord, Kaifi Azmi's compelling and poignant tribute to Nehru at the time of his funeral is etched in public memory.

Meri awaz suno, pyar ka saaz suno...
Kyun sajai hai yeh chandan ki chitah mere liye,
Mein koi jism nahin hun, ke jaladogey mujhe,
Raakh ke saath bikhar jaunga duniya mein,
Tum jahan khaoge thokar,wahin paoge mujhe...

A broad translation of the verse reads:

(Hear my voice, hear the music of love
Why have you set up this pyre for me?
I am not just a body that you can burn,

With my ashes, I will scatter myself across the world
Every time you stumble, you will find me beside
you…)

The poet, addressing the people through Nehru, conveys the immortality of his hero's vision and an assurance of the leader's guardianship of his people beyond life.

On the occasion of Pandit Nehru's 61st death anniversary and considering the troubled times that we live in, we must recall the poetic tribute of Atal Bihari Vajpayee at the time of Pandit-ji's passing. The veteran leader of the BJP had, with his usual eloquence, said about Nehru: "It was a dream, which merged into infinity … a flame of lamp, which kept burning through the night, fighting every darkness, and by showing us the way, itself attained nirvana one morning…"

The exceptionality of Nehru's leadership thus established, his resting place is assured in the pantheon of the great. The light of his vision, the power of his grace, the gentleness of his spirit, the strength of his conviction and the endless sacrifices he made for the country's freedom have justly earned him the veneration of his people. Jawaharlal Nehru introduced the "tone of modesty" and dignity at the centre of politics, repurposing it beyond the pursuit of power for its own sake. For all these reasons and more, Nehru's transformative leadership will remain an unending inspiration for generations to come. Hopefully, those who claim to pursue his legacy will not fail their idol.

Thank You, Doctor Sahib[2]

Manmohan Singh remained above the harshness of politics and the cold power games around him.

---

2. *Outlook Magazine* (Hindi), 31 December 2024; *Indian Express*, 2 January 2025; *Daily Ajit* (Punjabi), 2 January 2025.

A truly suitable eulogy to Dr Manmohan Singh is beyond my competence. This tribute to him can hardly do justice to the greatness of an extraordinary man whose life was marked by decency, integrity, humility and magnanimity. As the architect of India's economic reforms, he set the trajectory for the nation's rise as an Asian economic power and lifted millions of Indians above abject poverty. These contributions will remain a lasting testament to his vision and wisdom.

Singh's leadership role on the global high table in shaping the contours of the future world order amidst the transformational changes of our times makes the nation proud. Those who derided him for being "weak" need only recall his steely resolve in clinching the Indo-US Civil Nuclear Deal that ended India's nuclear apartheid and established the nation's credentials as a responsible nuclear power. The forging of what has now blossomed into an all-encompassing Special Strategic Global Partnership with Japan—seen as establishing an arc of peace and prosperity in Asia—is a tribute to his statesmanship and an incisive understanding of the realities of geopolitics.

After appointing me as his Special Envoy to Japan for facilitating the historic visit to India of their Imperial Majesties—the then Emperor and Empress of Japan—he told me that this was one of the most important state visits to our country and the Indo-Japan relationship was the defining bilateral partnership of the 21st century. Subsequent events have vindicated his vision. The record of his spectacular achievements as prime minister will not be complete without reference to his path-breaking initiatives and rights-based pieces of legislation such as MGNREGA, RTE, RTI, and the Farmers' Loan waiver. His tenure will also be remembered for the foundational framework of Aadhaar and the largest-ever budgetary allocations for education and healthcare.

His patience and forbearance in the face of grave provocation by allies and opponents secured the longevity of the government and ensured the political stability necessary for implementing the nation's ambitious development agenda. He saw and scripted the progressive future of our nation and seized upon the idea of a developed India whose time had come.

The unending accolades received by Singh, including from his vocal critics, affirm his towering stature amongst the world's foremost leaders. This is because of his innate humanity, selflessness, unimpeachable personal integrity and genuine concern for the welfare of all. The generosity of his heart made no exceptions. He could instinctively relate to the pain of others. None who came to him for assistance or solace in moments of despair left without being comforted. His was a healing touch, one that was both humbling and ennobling. He remained above the harshness of politics and the cold power games orchestrated around him.

In informal conversations, he would often mention the transience of power and, perhaps, therefore, carried the authority of his high office with a lightness of touch. At a difficult time during the UPA II, when some of his ministerial colleagues unfairly derided him, he refused to crack the whip, saying that he did not wish to discipline them as a headmaster. His rare reprimands to his ministers were softly delivered. Those who see this as a weakness must know that his life and politics were a reflection of his spirituality anchored in compassion and an abiding faith in the goodness of people.

Even as he navigated the treacherous pathways of politics, Singh did not allow his moral clarity to be diminished. He was deeply saddened by the allegations of corruption during the UPA II and agonised over his name "being dragged in the mud".

In moments of intense anxiety and extreme despair, such as in the last days of my late wife, he lent his shoulder as a family elder and comforted me. I recall his telephone call to tell me that "miracles are known to happen". That was his way of keeping my hopes alive.

On another occasion, when he had to cancel his presence at my son's wedding reception on account of last-minute security issues, he instructed several members of his personal staff in the PMO to represent him and his wife, Gursharan Kaur, who was his greatest source of strength. At the end of my last meeting with him, a little before Diwali in October this year, when I took leave of him, he patted me on my shoulder with a smile on his lips as if he was bidding me goodbye with his last blessings. This moment is etched in my consciousness, as are several other memories of his benevolence and grace that have given me a perpetual purpose in life—the pursuit of human dignity in all its manifestations.

Thank you, Doctor Sahib. And thank you, Sonia-ji, for giving us an outstanding prime minister who elevated himself above his exalted office.

Farewell Sir! Rest assured that history is kinder to you, your place assured in its annals, in the pantheon of the great. For the sceptics, let me invoke the felicity of the celebrated poet, Mir Taqi Mir, as a tribute to our beloved "Doctor Sahib".

Mat sehl hamein jano, phirta hai falak barson,
Tab khaak ke parde se, insaan nikalte hain

(Do not make the mistake of treating us as
unknowing/ordinary
For the skies wander for years, only then, from the
cloak of dust,
[such] human beings emerge.)

Saluting Dignity in Leadership[3]

May the light of your work for a better world shine forever.

3. Published in The *Asian Age* and *Deccan Chronicle* on 12 July 2022.

8 July 2022 was a day of colossal tragedy, when Prime Minister Shinzo Abe, Abe-san to his countless admirers across the world, was felled by the dastardly act of an assassin. The outrageous crime underscores the reality of a world torn by countless conflicts and faltering in its quest for a harmonious global order. The shocking loss of a "towering statesman" in these difficult times is without recompense and has dented our collective endeavour to establish a benign and humane world order founded on justice and human dignity. The vision of such a world and its relentless pursuit will remain the defining distinction of Abe-san's politics and personality.

As the longest-serving three-time prime minister of Japan, his tireless exertions to promote global peace and stability have left an indelible imprint across the world. His vision of a peaceful Indo-Pacific region as an "arc of freedom and prosperity", shared by Indian leaders cutting across party lines, resulted in a mutually reinforcing relationship between the two democracies. Prime Minister Abe's historic speech to the Indian Parliament in 2007, popularly referred to as "Confluence of the Two Seas", dwelt upon the complementarities between our nations. This visit laid the foundation of what the then Prime Minister Dr Manmohan Singh described as a "defining bilateral relationship of the 21st century".

The continuing momentum of the engagement between India and Japan resulted in what was officially declared a "Special Strategic and Global Partnership" in 2014, when Prime Minister Modi visited Japan in September of that year.

The ongoing phase of this unique partnership has seen the conclusion of strategically significant understandings between the two countries, including the historic "Agreement for Cooperation in Peaceful Uses of Nuclear Energy." Arrangements for enhanced maritime cooperation, strategic connectivity in the Indo-Pacific (Sri-Lanka, Myanmar, Bangladesh, and Africa), cooperation agreements against piracy, terrorism, and joint commitment to nuclear non-proliferation have enlarged the ambit of the relationship. The cementing of US-India-Japan trilateral defence cooperation which led to a quadrilateral grouping including Australia, joint naval exercises in the Malabar, Mine warfare and JIMEX (2018), the "Two Plus Two" dialogue between the foreign and defence ministers of India and Japan, the Annual Defence Ministerial Dialogue, Defence Policy Dialogue, National Security Advisors Dialogue,

Acquisition and Cross Servicing Agreement have vastly extended the reach of the India-Japan entente. Japan's support for India's membership of the Nuclear Suppliers Group and reform of the UN, particularly of the UNSC, underscores the depth of the partnership.

It is for all these reasons and more that there exists a special bond between Abe-san and the Indian people. My tribute to an illustrious son of Japan will not be complete without the recording of personal recollections of Abe-san's deep sense of humility, honour and warmth that defined him.

My association with him began in 2007 when I was appointed as his accompanying minister for the duration of his state visit to India that year. In this capacity, I was part of his entourage from the moment he arrived in India till his departure, and therefore, had the opportunity of observing him from close quarters.

During the visit, Prime Minister Abe was suffering from an acute stomach ailment, because of which his hectic official schedule was adjusted to give him a few minutes of personal time and relief between back-to-back meetings. I could sense from his facial expression an acute sense of unease and discomfort, which he never expressed, lest it interrupt the schedule of his official engagements.

Soon after returning to Japan at the height of his popularity, Prime Minister Abe tendered his resignation in September 2007. The visuals of his resignation on TV screens across the world have left an indelible imprint on people's minds. The sight of Japan's most powerful political figure announcing his resignation with a deep bow and majestically striding past his senior colleagues who stood in respect in an even deeper bow touched me to the depths of my being. Here was a unique example of a leader who, in an act of selflessness and answering the call of his conscience, chose to walk away from power and the global limelight. He did so again in August 2020 on account of a recurring ailment. The two deeply moving bows at the time of his resignations in 2007 and 2020 will forever remain etched in public memory as awe-inspiring gestures of duty, grace, honour, and dignity which defined the man and the statesman.

Moved by his resignation in 2007, I sought an appointment with him for a courtesy call during one of my official visits to Tokyo that year. I met Abe-san at his party office. This was an emotional meeting for me and lasted beyond the stipulated time. While taking leave of the former prime minister, I told him that I felt he was destined to return to lead his country once again as prime minister, which he did in 2012. Thereafter, I had occasions to meet him on the margins of the annual Kyoto conferences of the STS Forum, of which he was the patron. On these occasions, he would make it a point to speak a few words in English with me to indicate a personal bond. I also had the privilege of receiving and hosting him at my residence in New Delhi on one of his visits to India when he was not in office.

In 2013, I was appointed by Prime Minister Manmohan Singh as his Special Envoy to Japan to assist with preparations for the visit of the then Emperor and Empress of Japan to India. In this connection, I visited Tokyo and called on Prime Minister Abe to discuss arrangements for the royal visit. The cordial one-on-one meeting lasted beyond the stipulated time. The understated smile on his face conveyed the warmth that he felt for India and its importance in the realisation of a shared vision for global peace and prosperity.

In these troubled times, when the world needs statesmen to address the extraordinary challenges of our age, Shinzo Abe's departure from the world stage is an irreparable loss to a world seeking to reinvent itself for the better. Of the life and work of Prime Minister Abe, we can say without hesitation, in the words of historian E.H. Carr in another context, that he was "an outstanding individual who [was] at once a product and an agent of the historical process, at once the representative and creator of the social forces which changed the shape of the world and the thoughts of men". He was not only the leader of his country but was a leader of the times.

Farewell, Abe-san, on your last journey and may the light of your work for a better world shine forever.

INDEX

B

C

D

E

F

G

H

N

O

P

R

S

T

U

V

W

Y

Z

ACKNOWLEDGEMENTS

I acknowledge with gratitude the assistance rendered by my diligent colleagues, advocates Shefali Sangwan, Shourya Tiwari, Anmol Gupta and Komal Pathak in carrying out the necessary editorial corrections and formatting of the book. A deep debt of gratitude is due to Professor Upendra Baxi and S. Prasannarajan for their most valuable inputs. Above all, thanks are due to the esteemed publications that have done me the honour of publishing the opinion pieces in their columns. Thanks to Harini Srinivasan for introducing me to Om Books International. I would like to thank Shantanu Ray Chaudhuri and Shreya Kumari for their meticulous work on the text in double quick time, and Sheena Gupta for turning in the cover. I am greatly indebted to my publisher, Ajay Mago. Thanks to Manjari Chaturvedi and Harini Srinivasan for introducing me to Om Books International.